Go for it with passion.

Michael

"If you invest in just one business book this year, this should be it. Packed with solid advice and inspiring true-to-life stories, Leading High Impact Teams is a practical blueprint for revolutionizing your organization."
—Peter Whitford, Chairman, Whitmark Corporation; Former President, Structure, Inc.

"Never steering you in the wrong direction, this book charts the course for creating and sustaining high impact teams. Through real-life scenarios, practical worksheets and tips, and working with my Coach, this book helped provide me with the foundation I needed to create a high impact team."
—Lois Wortley, Director of Product Management, Oracle Corporation

"Speaking from a background rich in relevant experience, the authors have carefully articulated the principles required to turn a business from static to electric! This book should be required reading for every team member and executive in every organization. It will coach you in becoming an outstanding coach for your team while getting much better results!"
—Sandy Vilas, CEO, Coach U

"Amidst the myriad types of advice in the business marketplace, the principles of coaching are shaping the ways in which business is done effectively. This book is a timely and eminently practical guide to applying coaching to jumpstart teams and produce exceptional results."
—Jean Hamilton, CEO Prudential Institutional, EVP Prudential Financial

"For me, coaching is an attitude. It means, 'I am your boss but I am in this with you. I am here to help you be your best so we can attain our mutual goals together.' As the skipper of five America's Cup teams and one Whitbread Around the World campaign, I have some experience in leading teams. However, I am constantly trying to raise my game. Leading High Impact Teams gives a comprehensive look at the role of the coach in an organization. I found its approach to be right on the money, as well as inspiring and educational."
—Paul Cayard, CEO & Skipper, AmericaOne

"*Leading High Impact Teams is the most comprehensive and practical book I've read in more than twenty years of working with teams. I look forward to using the insights and exercises with all my clients.*"

—Marcia Reynolds, M.A., M.Ed., MCC., author of *Being In the Zone* and *Capture the Rapture*, Recent Past President, International Coach Federation

"*Fantastic reading with valuable insight for executive managers building a high impact team.*"

—George Nolen, President & CEO, Siemens Enterprise Networks LLC

"*Corporate America had better heed the coaching phenomenon, even if it falls outside the traditional corporate organizational chart.*"

—*Fortune* Magazine, article featuring author Cynder Niemela

"*A terrific primer that every team leader should have on their bookshelf. This is the book you will reach for when something's not quite working in your team. It can be a challenge to keep teams functioning all the time; when things aren't going 100%, this book will identify the process that's missing!*"

—Mark Keough, Vice President, Monster Learning, Monster.com

"*This book is well written and easy to understand. I have used and benefited from many of the strategies taught here. My employees, peers, and supervisors have acknowledged me for using new and fun techniques in working with others. Wow!*"

—Cindy Overton, District Manager, Radio Shack

"*When I first met Cynder and Rachael, I knew they had something special, as if they had written the book on coaching teams. Well, now they have, and what a masterpiece it is! Their depth of experience is clearly reflected and provides a great road map for anyone who wants to get the most out of their teams!*"

—David Goldsmith, President, CoachInc.com

"*Cynder Niemela and Rachael Lewis are a knock-out combo of executive coaches who have produced a clear guide for corporations to use to create high impact teams! Team Coaches are becoming a common resource for global organizations as businesses expand and evolve in dynamic environments. This book is a how-to guide that makes team coaching a tangible and facilitative process.*"

—D. J. Mitsch, CMC, MCC, President, Pyramid Resource Group,
President, The International Coach Federation

"*This book shows you a much more effective way to create outstanding teams: The Coach Approach! If you are a coach, leader or anyone that develops teams, this book will give you hints, practical skills, and the right questions to ask your team at every stage of the journey. If you want to use coaching skills to develop your team, this book is perfect for you.*"

—Michael Göthe, Competence Manager and Team Coach, Ericsson Spain

"*Leading High Impact Teams provides a great set of principles and practices for building and coaching high perfomance teams. The new distinctions will contribute greatly to your knowledge and wisdom about teams.*"

—Carl Zaiss, Carl Zaiss International, Inc., Co-author of *Sales Effectiveness Training*

"*There's a wealth of wisdom in this book, and I highly recommend it. Rachael and Cynder are expert team coaches, and they have distilled years of experience into an immensely practical book. This is an applied, hands-on approach, exactly what's needed for working with business teams today.*"

—Dr. Joel M. Rothaizer, Executive/Team Coach and Organizational
Development Consultant, CEO, Clear Impact Consulting Group, Inc.

"*Today's leading organizations are achieving breakthrough results by skillfully combining two performance drivers: the power of teams, supplemented by expert team coaching. In this masterpiece Cynder and Rachael show you how to achieve great results in ways that build both human capital and the human spirit!*"

—Chuck Bolton, Founder, The Bolton Group,
Former Group Vice President, Human Resources, Boston Scientific Corporation

Leading
High Impact Teams

The Coach Approach
To Peak Performance

by

Cynder Niemela and Rachael Lewis

Order additional copies
and bulk orders (for your leaders and teams) from:

High Impact Publishing
668 North Coast Highway #188
Laguna Beach CA 92651
866-HI TEAMS phone
(866-448-3267)
www.HighImpactTeams.com
Discounts available for bulk purchases

Niemela, Cynder.
Leading high impact teams : the coach approach to peak performance / Cynder Niemela
and Rachael Lewis — 1st ed.
p. cm.
Includes bibliographical references and index.
ISBN: 0-9710888-0-2
1. Teams in the workplace. 2. Performance. 3. Leadership.
I. Lewis, Rachael. II. Title
HD66.N54 2001 658.402
QB101-200677

Cover by Steve Graydon
Interior design by Sara L. Greenfield, Art Squad Graphics
Printed in U.S.A.

First edition

10   9   8   7   6   5   4   3   2   1

Table of Contents

Acknowledgments

This book is a result of the encouragement, support, inspiration and love of numerous people. To all of you, and those whom we may have forgotten to mention, a heartfelt thank you for your guidance and love over the past two years since the inception of the idea.

David Goldsmith of CoachInc.com recognized the amazing possibility of our collaboration and introduced us to each other. That was the start of our journey as partners. David, Sandy Vilas, and Thomas Leonard, the brainpower and guts behind Coach U, gave us the opportunity to develop and present our material for the coaches and leaders at Coach U and Corporate Coach U. Distinctions throughout the book are sourced from their body of knowledge.

We are grateful for the courage and endorsement of our clients who have partnered with us in their growth and development as leaders in their work and in their lives. A special thank you to Richard Buck, Sarah Howarth, Donna Dyer, Laurette Mormon, and Barry Mabry for your willingness to take precious time to share your stories with the media.

To Elizabeth Danziger of WorkTalk.com for masterful guidance and sharp wit in taking our concepts, tales, and tools helping us to get to the point. We couldn't have done this without you.

Lee Smith and Jeanine Sandstrom have been generous, gracious and powerful models for us, as team and executive coaches. We thank them for their significant contributions to the corporate coaching community. We particularly cherish our collaboration with Jan Austin and are grateful for her willingness to share her gift of language with us to make this book fantastic.

To Ernst & Young, who believed in coaching for themselves and also for their clients, thank you for the support to innovate the coach approach in developing high impact teams.

To *Fortune* magazine and expert interviewer Betsy Morris, who helped spread the word about the unique benefits of having an executive coach on your team.

To our precious first wise women coaches Harriett Simon Salinger, Delores Madgett, and Lyn Allen. Without a doubt, you masterfully brought out our best to embark on this kaleidoscopic journey by seeing our lives and our work through previously unrecognized filters.

Dawson Church of Authors Publishing Cooperative, we could not pull off this octopus of a project without your marketing and distribution wizardry. Anne Ferguson kept us on track and the details in order as an expert virtual assistant.

From Rachael . . .

I give a special thanks to Elizabeth Carrington, an inspiration in her own right, who beckons me over life's roadblocks ever so caringly. To Brook Cross, Jim Vollett, J.R. Miller, Lee Weinstein, Dr.

Joel Rothaizer—all my coaching colleagues and friends—thank you for your endless support. And to my early mentors in the corporate world, Jim Carmody and Luke Brown, who really taught me what it meant to grow people beyond where they thought they could go themselves. What a lesson it's been!

Most importantly, I send my love and thanks to my parents and brothers. Without you beside me, this would not be possible. I am humbled by your generous, loving support.

For the grace and cheerleading of my cross-country community of courageous women—Eileen, Suzanne, Sophia, Rinatta, Kathy, Cynthia and Christy—hallelujah!

From Cynder . . .

The willingness of my family, friends and clients to set aside their own priorities and help me not only felt great, but resulted in a much better product. I especially want to thank my caring husband, Mark Niemela, whose support and love have created a safe place for my growth. He never seemed to grow tired of asking —or prodding—me about how our book was going. Thank you, Mark, for your patience, your willingness to remain interested and encouraging, and, even if you may have had doubts as to whether or not we'd finish this book, for keeping your thoughts to yourself.

Maintaining a balance between work and family is an important value for me. While I consider family and personal relationships a central purpose of my life, there were times in writing this book that my behavior indicated otherwise. I appreciate everyone's tolerance and support. And now that this book is finished, I know that my family, friends and clients share in its accomplishment. I trust that this work makes a contribution to improving the quality of all our lives.

About the Authors

How do we know that the Coach Approach to developing high impact teams works? We have implemented it in a variety of industries with companies such as Lucent Technologies, Hewlett-Packard, Oracle Corporation, Ernst & Young, and Northern Light Technology, as well as many other small, medium and large organizations. We've coached teams through acquisitions, new product development projects, large-scale business application initiatives, and culture change initiatives. Together, we've coached over 100 organizations and individuals in the past 20 years.

The need for strong leadership in business, government and society has never been greater. Beyond conventional wisdom and servant leadership, today's leaders must focus on developing practices, behaviors, attitudes and values that energize people and their organizations. We aim to create cohesiveness and shared commitment among executives and team members, thus helping teams achieve a real competitive advantage. We work closely with clients to generate and implement a development plan that targets specific strengths and shortcomings. Client companies hire coaches to address these objectives:

- develop high impact teams
- enhance organizational financial health
- leverage organizational change and chaos
- strengthen relationships and minimize performance issues
- enhance communications and balance personal and professional life
- develop the talent of new or seasoned leaders

Cynder Niemela, Managing Partner, VISTA COACH, is a Professional Certified Coach (PCC) with Masters' degrees in business and psychology and more than 20 years experience in coaching executives and business teams worldwide. Cynder implements technologies and processes that are far more challenging and long-term than traditional mentoring and consulting. She coaches executives to effectively lead key members and whole teams to achieve exceptional results. Her clients are innovative, proactive leaders and professionals who are dedicated to living their dreams.

As an internal and external coach with Ernst & Young Consulting Group, Cynder specialized in the coach approach to building high impact teams to support major business transformations.

As noted in a recent *Fortune* magazine article, "So You're a Player; Do You Need a Coach?" Cynder's skills and expertise have inspired executives from major firms like Ernst & Young to achieve both team and individual goals. Among her other clients are Lucent Technologies, Hewlett-Packard, 3Com Corporation, Oracle Corporation, and Seagate Technology.

Rachael Lewis, Principal, Trilogy Coaching Institute, brings over 14 years of business experience in the technology, retail, and hospitality industries managing geographically and culturally diverse teams. Her primary focus is on helping individuals and teams thrive in the workplace while producing breakthrough results. In her coaching practice, she has worked with many teams as they made significant transitions such as mergers and acquisitions.

Rachael is known as a compassionate straight-talker who shares insightful feedback and co-develops pragmatic remedies that challenge her clients. As a Team Coach, she works with team leaders and team members to raise their level of interpersonal and technical competency, to see and surpass their obstacles, and to adopt a more focused, strategic approach to being effective. Rachael also works with executives and managers to develop the professional and personal mastery to meet company objectives with a balanced work life. Rachael's clients appreciate her keen intuition, evocative questions, and attention to process and progress that have helped them go much further than they had ever expected.

Rachael's corporate coaching and training clients include mid and senior level managers and teams at companies such as Oracle Corporation, Northern Light Technology, MAI Systems Corporation, Deep Ocean Odyssey, T3 Media and others.

Rachael and Cynder are both faculty members and co-developers of the Coaching Business Teams teleclass for Corporate Coach U. In addition, they are both graduates of and faculty members at Coach U. They are Master Facilitators for The Coaching Clinic and they are among the first to be certified as Professional Certified Coaches by the International Coach Federation (ICF). Rachael is President and founder of the Orange County (California) chapter of the ICF and is an active member of the American Society for Training and Development. Cynder is the current Chairperson of the Organizational Coaching Committee of the ICF.

For our online newsletter, e-mail: subscribe@highimpactteams.com. You can contact the authors at:

High Impact Teams
www.HighImpactTeams.com
866-HI TEAMS (448-3267)

Foreword

One night a six-year-old girl asked her father, "Daddy, why can't Mommy play with me after dinner? Why does she always have to go to the study and get on the computer?" The father responded, "Well, honey, your mother can't always get all of her work done during the day, so she has to do it after dinner." The girl looked carefully at her father and, in her infinite wisdom, said, "But Daddy, if she can't get her work done during the day, why don't they put her in a slower group?"

The pace of work in America and throughout the world has accelerated at an amazing rate in the past twenty years—so much so, that change and an increase in pace and pressure within organizations are the only constant. Competition has increased, and new markets have opened so quickly, that the way in which we go about our lives has fundamentally shifted. Slow groups no longer exist, only accelerating ones. This is important because with this increased pressure towards productivity and profitability, companies are forced to fundamentally change the way people are organized and the way they are managed.

Organizations have been looking to team structures and increased teamwork to meet the new demands of today's pressure cooker business environment. In a recent survey of Fortune 500 CEOs, the number one issue facing these leaders "is the creation of a team based culture."

Teams enable groups of people to respond more effectively and creatively to challenges than do traditional structures. Teams foster involvement, cooperation, creativity, fun and dialogue . . . critical elements for success.

Yet while teams are an exciting way to organize people at work, they come with a hefty cost. Teams are tough to manage in the best of circumstances, and are a nightmare if only a few things go wrong. The world of professional sports provides an excellent example. So often the team with the most talent is unable to live up to their potential because of bad chemistry. Case in point: the Los Angeles Lakers, a team with amazing talent for the past five years, was unable to find success. Despite having a cast of stars including Shaquille O'Neil and Kobe Bryant, the Lakers were a regular disappointment in the playoffs. What caused the shift in the 1999–2000 season to league champions? A great coach, Phil Jackson, was the answer. Phil was able to take this same group of men, and turn them into incredible champions.

Great coaching equals great teams. Coaching, a known commodity in the sports world, is increasingly used as an effective means for leading teams in the world of business. Coaching today is a far cry from the hard-nosed tactics of classic football coaches. Instead it draws the wisdom, experience and passion out of each individual on a team as it pursues a clear and important mission. Great coaching draws on the individual members to take responsibility for the results of the team.

When Cynder and Rachael asked me to write this foreword, I was really excited. I am a tremendous believer in both coaching and team work, as they are two of the most powerful trends which have emerged in organizations over the past two years.

As I got into the book, I was struck by how masterfully coaching was articulated in the context of teams. At their best, teams are tricky and murky to manage; at worst they can be disastrous. Few of us are able to make the shift from a team member or a traditional manager to a team coach. Cynder and Rachael provide countless insightful distinctions and a new way to consider teams.

Throughout the book I learned not only about changes in attitude and skills that must be made for an individual to be effective in a team environment, but also about who we must be and the fundamental place we must come from. The premise of a coach approach is that each person on a team understands and leverages the gifts, skills and strengths they naturally possess. Teams are truly effective when diverse resources and skills are combined to produce results far greater than those that could be produced individually.

Through the numerous examples, insights and activities provided, I gained tremendous confidence in the approach presented. The roles of all players on the team were laid out clearly in a way that caused me to feel increasing excitement and confidence in my ability to coach a team.

I have read most of the classic approaches to teams over the years as well as some of the new, breakthrough works on teams, none of which have provided me with a more complete approach to actually bringing teams to life. Although in my heart and mind, I had always known coaching and teams would combine into a powerful partnership, Cynder and Rachael further confirmed this in providing an extremely strong argument and process for reaching peak performance in your organization through well-coached teams!

Scott Blanchard
Founder and CEO
Coaching.com
May, 2001

Preface

The Workplace Imperative
In the Age of New Work

New work, as some have named it, is irrevocably changing the fabric of all organizations. Ready access to advanced technology, government deregulation, and customer demand for better products and services at lower prices have dramatically increased competition. Consumers have a dizzying array of choices in products that are produced all over the world. And, consumers have gotten smarter. They understand clearly that they can expect increasingly better deals—and get them. Organizations, if they are to survive, much less thrive, must play by these new rules, and the implications are profound. New imperatives are on the agenda:

- Deliver extraordinary value to customers for a competitive price
- Cut product and service costs and reduce manufacturing cycle times

- Innovate, innovate, innovate, because the competition isn't waiting
- Simplify work processes so that all work performed is high impact work
- Delegate decision making and direct information that is critical to decision making to those closest to the customer
- Develop the skills of everyone in the organization to work collaboratively in teams designed to address critical organizational issues and deliver high impact results
- Retain the top talent you attract by nurturing an intrinsically motivating environment

Addressing these imperatives requires nothing short of revamping the way work has been performed for most of the 20th century. The rigid bureaucracy of the traditional workplace must give way to new structures which encourage timely decision making at all levels of the organization, and foster just-in-time learning. It must promote innovation by those working most closely with products and services. Flatter organizational structures, downsizing, and increased emphasis on lean production processes demand that every worker in today's organization have the hard and soft skills to do a variety of tasks. They are called upon to engage in creative problem solving about work processes, given opportunities for innovation, and required to *work with others* to accomplish that which cannot be accomplished alone. In short, workers must become much more capable of *self-directed teamwork.*

Many of us have not developed strong teamwork skills, and most groups of people who try to work as "teams" in organizations end up floundering. There are a number of reasons for this:

Individual accomplishment, not teamwork, has been the mainstay of most organizational recognition and reward systems. Power and prestige have been limited to those at the very top of the organization, with others playing supporting roles, and requiring daily direction from those at the top.

Teamwork requires different attitudes and different communi-cation skills. The attitude of "me first" doesn't fit with the notion of shared purposes and shared responsibility for achieving results. Moreover, communication in groups requires a high level of attention. It requires constructive responses to the diversity represented by other team members' backgrounds, communication styles, job roles, cultural context and other factors.

Traditional work systems designs have organized work into "com-ponents." The best example of this is the assembly line. In an assembly line, workers work on their assigned components, but do not have an appreciation for the whole picture. From this vantage point, they have not been expected to engage in creative problem solving or input into how work is performed. Multiple layers of supervisors and managers have been in place to make these decisions.

Workers of the past had more of the knowledge needed to per-form their jobs. The typical worker of two decades ago had 80% or more of the knowledge needed to do his or her job right at his or her fingertips. But today's fast-paced, information-driven environment is serving up more information than at any time in history. The typical worker now has less than 20% of the knowledge needed to do the job. This has driven the need for higher levels of interdependence—people working together—to accomplish the work.

The workplace imperatives in the age of new work are clear and compelling. Everyone has to work differently if the organization is to survive and thrive. Workers have to be more collaborative and engage as members of high impact teams. It is incumbent upon leaders and coaches to go first—to develop the requisite attitudes, skills and behaviors, and to stand up as models of excellence for others to follow. The stakes are very high indeed, but the opportunities have never been more abundant.

—Jan Austin
Certified Corporate Coach
Coach to Teams and Team Leaders

Introduction

Tiger Woods would say, "I know how to play golf," but his coach is probably the most important person in his life.

—Barry Mabry, *Ernst & Young Partner*
Fortune magazine

Leading High Impact Teams: The Coach Approach to Peak Performance is a timely resource for everyone who coaches or leads organizational teams charged with delivering high impact results. High impact results—those that deliver the greatest value to the customer for the most competitive price—are the only results that count in today's marketplace.

Leading High Impact Teams is written drawing on a coach approach. The coach approach can be simply and elegantly described as the ways and means by which people's passion for possibility is unleashed. The coach approach assumes that every organizational team member has the potential to leverage his or her strengths for the achievement of world-class business results. The voice of the coach in this book is intentional. It serves as an affirmation of the need for every leader to adopt a role that serves as a catalyst for others to step up, stretch, and realize their potential.

Leading High Impact Teams assists the team leader or coach in responding to the frequent challenges every team experiences, and which can be heard in the following typical comments from team leaders and members:

- "We have all these meetings but nothing ever seems to get done."
- "We have teams but no teamwork."
- "We don't talk to each other; we talk at each other."
- "We come to agreement on how to proceed and then we don't follow through."
- "I have responsibility for a big team and I've never been here before."
- "We are way behind schedule, and people aren't getting along."
- "I've been given the feedback that I am ineffective at delegating."
- "I'm working at 110% capacity, and I can't keep it up."

Leading High Impact Teams incorporates an imaginative array of assessments, methods, activities and questions to promote the attitudes and behaviors that are vital to effective and enjoyable teamwork. Both new and experienced team coaches and leaders will find much to support and enhance their work with both newly organizing and existing teams.

- **Assessments** are provided to pinpoint the team's strengths and opportunities for improvement.
- **Activities** are provided to support the design of effective teamwork sessions.
- **Anecdotes** are sprinkled throughout because we learn more easily from stories.
- **Case Stories** at the end of each chapter demonstrate the use of coaching in a variety of real team situations.

- **Distinctions** are provided to enhance the team's ability to take more discerning actions.
- **Inquiries** are meant to provoke deeper understanding and integration of new ideas.

Although the stories and anecdotes are all real, we have not included company or individual names in order to honor our agreement of confidentiality with our clients.

Finally, *Leading High Impact Teams* explores the phases of team development, including the predictable obstacles that arise as teams pass through natural stages. Each chapter of the book offers the reader an overview of the role of the coach during that phase, specific activities the coach or leader can use with the team, and case stories that integrate the concepts presented.

Use this book as a resource and field guide. Use it to grow your skills as a team leader and coach, and use these skills to support others to be extraordinary in their work as team members. Most of all, bring your passion for people and teams right into the room, and be a model of all that team membership can be!

We invite you to share with us your wins and your challenges. E-mail us at coach@highimpactteams.com.

Enjoy yourself. Stay passionate!

PART I

WHO'S WHO:

Coach, Captain
and Crew

CHAPTER 1

The Role of the Coach: Preparing to Coach Your Team

Listening is a magnetic and strange thing, a creative force.
The people who listen to us are the ones we move toward.
When we are listened to, it creates us, and makes
us unfold and expand.

—Karl Menninger

You would think that a 138% increase in revenue comes from working at least 50% harder. In fact, the first high impact team we're going to introduce you to works no harder than before. Life is not a struggle and staff turnover is 0%—far from the company norm of 34%. While other teams in this organization are churning in rough seas, this team has decisively disembarked from the burnout cruise.

Let's meet Steve Boyes, a partner in a global financial services firm and the leader of this team. Here's how he explains his success: "Since adding a coach to our team, our time spent relating with each other has increased dramatically. Never before was this the norm in our consulting firm. The focus of meetings was always on projects, tasks and issues.

"It says in our company's vision statement that we are expected to develop long-term relationships with our clients. Relationships are supposed to provide ongoing client engagements and increased revenues. But, historically, we gave ourselves no time to create— much less develop—even superficial relationships with the members of our own team. If our team of consultants is not cohesive, then how can we possibly team *with* our clients? We had to confront this paradox, and our team did.

"Within three months of initiating a coach approach, our clients started reaping the benefits of the synergy of our team. An immediate benefit was improved team cohesion. Team members discovered a new sense of connection through meaningful conversations. In a recent meeting, heartfelt concerns were expressed for a team member who is facing major surgery. And although the team is geographically dispersed, we make time to get together for outings to concerts and baseball games.

"We've become creative in solving customer problems. Who would have believed that in this buttoned-down, facts-are-facts consulting company, we'd be wearing colored hats to represent the persona of another team member as we brainstorm a cost-effective, innovative solution to a mind-boggling problem? Having experienced deep, meaningful relationships with each other, we now understand how to build strong relationships and strong teams *within* client companies. *I hate to admit it, but the rest—revenue, turnover, and morale—has taken care of itself.*"

• • •

Prior to the start of coaching, Steve was lamenting the situation of his team. Every three years he makes a habit of evaluating whether or not he wants to sign up for another three years at his firm. He acknowledges that he loves his work, his clients and his firm. But times have changed and so has the culture of the firm. During his last pause for reflection, after 20 years on the job, he was not so sure that he would find the next three years as satisfying.

Constant change, high turnover, and fluctuating revenue were taking a toll on his motivation. He was no longer authorized to reward his team members with pay raises or promotions. Plus, if he didn't improve his financial performance, he might become the next candidate for a pink slip.

We started our coaching by helping Steve discover the source of his dissatisfaction. Then we explored his opportunities before deciding on a course of action. Steve said, "I want to give my people something I haven't been able to give them in the past. What can I do to cause a genuine turnaround of morale, and motivate them to show up at work when the resources aren't available that I used to give?"

Steve and his team were good candidates for high impact team coaching. Steve is a motivated leader who wanted a new way to inspire his team. In this environment of change and turmoil, he knew he needed to find a new way of leading if his team was to thrive. Steve envisioned leading his team in a way that would empower the team to produce better results in a high-pressure environment, and bring him renewed satisfaction.

The coaching program lasted one year. Coaching sessions were conducted both in person and virtually by teleconference. The High Impact Team Assessment (see Chapter 3) was administered to uncover team strengths, as well as opportunities for improvement. Our strategy was to leverage the team's strengths, while also shoring up the areas in which they needed the most help.

The results of the High Impact Team Assessment were disheartening. Trust among team members was rare. They held no inspiring vision. Other teams were not supporting their work. But they had some things working in their favor. They reported that they were clear about their roles and responsibilities. Performance targets were agreed upon. They held themselves accountable for the work of the team. They also agreed that they were reasonably competent when running meetings, making decisions, and solving problems.

In our first team session, the team identified three objectives for coaching. The first was to increase trust. The group acknowledged that they worked in a competitive environment. They tended to hold back their thoughts and feelings for fear of risking a promotion, a positive evaluation, or being chosen for a project.

We began our coaching by giving them an assignment. They were asked to identify language that fostered trust, and language that eroded trust. They were asked to observe and report how leaders could foster collaboration through language.

The second coaching objective was to develop relatedness on the team. We first conducted a communication style assessment. Team members began to appreciate how their differences fit together like an intricate puzzle, and how this complementarity helped manifest the team's vision.

After a session spent working on this issue, one team member reported, "It's not bad to think I am a personality. It helps me understand how I interact with others." Another said, "As a peacemaker, it does my heart good to hear you talking about pulling together." In effect, team members shifted from thinking of themselves as a group of individual contributors to seeing themselves as a collection of strengths.

Setting up a shared vision was their third objective. They boiled it down to two powerful words: Excellent service. As a new year approached, they upped the ante and revised their vision. Their new vision statement is: Excellent innovative service for our clients and a balanced life for every member of our team.

They followed a journey from low to high impact that parallels the journey described in this book. As of this writing, this team is a shining star in an organization that is trying to recover from a series of layoffs, a merger, and a slump in revenues. In the first letters of appreciation they've ever received, clients have acknowledged the team's proactive approach in delivering innovative solutions despite constantly changing financial needs. Team members have been publicly recognized in the organization for their exemplary personal service.

At the start of the new year, as he pondered his next three years, Steve wholeheartedly chose to continue in his leadership role. "We've been equipped with a process to leverage inevitable change and *sustain* peak performance," he told us. As coaches, we felt his words to be an acknowledgment that our work was complete.

• • •

In this chapter you will learn about the role of the coach and about core coaching skills. You will also learn how to distinguish the coach's role from that of team leader, team member, and other roles on the team. If you are a team leader who is adopting a "coach approach" to leadership, you will find this chapter particularly valuable in helping you develop your core coaching skills. Our underlying purpose is to help you empower teams to create sustainable change and increase the likelihood that they can repeat success in the future. To achieve this goal, you will coach the team to envision its future and to help team members develop skills and strategies to reach their destination.

People often ask us, "What does a coach *do?*" Prospective teams initially think that we are note takers, or that we will "correct" team members' behaviors when they can't. Or they may assume we'll do "team building exercises" that will fix all the team's ills so that it can magically become a high impact team. Those who have these expectations are sometimes disappointed to learn that this is not what we do. After working with us for a while, our clients realize that we have a definite role and a set of skills that produce real results. Team members come to understand that the coach does not do the team's work—the team members do. They know that the coach is not accountable for the team's business results—the team leader, along with the rest of the team, is accountable for business results.

When acting as a coach, your role may often be subtle or behind the scenes. The coach's role is similar to the role of a tactician on a ship. The tactician knows the ship's course and stays alert for factors that might speed or impede the ship's progress toward its destination. He might notice subtle environmental factors such as a change in the wind or the color of the sea, or interpersonal issues such as tension within the crew or between the crew and the officers. The tactician's understated interventions carry enormous leverage in the ultimate success of the journey. A tiny deviation from a ship's course early in the voyage can leave a ship miles off course in the end. Similarly, a coach helps business teams to stay on course. In asking powerful questions and in doing subtle interventions, a coach helps ease the team's progress toward its goal.

Team coaches value individual development as well as team success. Skillful team coaches help people develop confidence and competence to maneuver through future projects and challenges, not just the current project. The intent of team coaching is to focus on meeting organizational goals while simultaneously developing the human capital thereby preparing the organization to successfully meet future challenges.

> Coaching illuminates what has gone unseen.

Thus, the answer to the question, "What does a coach do?" is paradoxical. From one standpoint the coach doesn't do the team's work. Yet from another standpoint the coach is a pivotal part of the system that enables the team to succeed.

YOUR ROLE AS COACH

As coach, you work with the team leader to help create a safe environment for open and effective communication. In this safe environment, you challenge the team by telling the truth and asking questions based on your observations. You develop the leader's coaching competencies by paying close attention to how his behaviors, actions and words impact team members and business results. In the interactions between coach and leader and between coach and team, you model coaching skills. Your coaching helps a team sort through the complexities of doing its work to ensure that the outcome has a positive impact on other parts of the organization, its clients, and other stakeholders.

Because of your familiarity with a team's developmental process, you can begin work by helping team members understand the phases that teams naturally go through. You alert team members to anticipate the likely and normal hazard zones and to plan for them. In essence, you empower the leader and the team to intentionally chart the team's route throughout the journey. This in turn enables the leader to gain agreement from the team members about the group's chartered destination and how they will work together to be successful.

Many coaches find that maintaining an empowering rather than active role is the most difficult part of coaching. In order to help the team, the coach must restrain the urge to jump in and *do* something about the team's problems. The desire to fix, talk, and solve problems for others often obstructs not only the coach's ability to master the coaching process but also hinders the team's evolution into high performance.

At one company, we started working with a new project team. At the end of our second meeting, the executive group had a meeting scheduled and they asked us to stay and observe their meeting. We in turn asked them how they wanted us to participate. They asked us to observe and give them feedback later. The meeting had been called at the last minute to resolve an urgent problem.

Quickly the meeting seemed to go off course and become chaotic. "Obviously, what's needed here is an effective problem-solving approach where they clarify their objectives, concerns and successful outcomes," we thought. "We could jump in uninvited. We could say nothing and speak with the team after the meeting, or we could ask a guiding question during the meeting." We chose not to say anything because we didn't have permission to contribute and intervention wasn't part of the agreement of our participation.

The following week, our observations from the meeting was a topic on their meeting agenda. Our feedback was that we didn't observe an effective process for problem solving. We asked them if they wanted to improve their approach to problem solving. They agreed and we scheduled an activity to develop a team problem-solving process.

When team members first encounter you as their coach, they probably will not know what to expect from you. You might be brought in after the team's project is underway or you might be fortunate enough to work with the team members from the inception of the team. Either way, one of your first objectives will be to help them understand how to benefit most from your coaching. Only when both you and the team members are clear about your role as coach, can you set sail. We discuss in more detail how to clarify and establish your role with a team in Chapter 5.

YOUR JOURNEY WITH A TEAM AS COACH

A coach's role is to help the team understand its journey. It is equally important for you as the coach to have a clear idea of what the journey with the team will be like. In the following ten chapters, we will provide you with coaching strategies, activities, and guidance for each step along the journey. Some key elements of the journey are:

- Contracting with the team to define its purpose, goals, operating instructions and commitment for the coaching engagement.
- Clarifying the leader's objectives for the team and for the coaching.
- Assessing the phase of evolution the team is in when you are brought on board and throughout the journey; also team strengths, and opportunities for improvement.
- Developing a plan of coaching activities to match your findings and the goals of the coaching engagement.
- Coaching the team and the team leader.
- Coaching team members individually.
- Coaching the team to a successful conclusion of its work.
- Completing the coaching assignment with the sponsor, the team, the leader and yourself.

CORE BUSINESS TEAM COACHING SKILLS

The goal of team coaching is to help a group of people with a common purpose identify and meet business goals and simultaneously enjoy the journey as a team. A masterful coach uses the following skills to clarify the discovered outcomes, develop a plan of action, and overcome the barriers along the way. These are the foundational skills of a masterful coach.

Accountability

Accountability is having people be responsible to themselves and to others for what they say they are going to do. A coach helps create a culture of accountability by holding people accountable to their vision and commitments. A coach asks people to account for the results of the intended action and if need be, define new actions to be taken. Accountability is determined by posing three questions: *What are you going to do? When will you do this? How will I know?*

Acknowledgment

Acknowledgment is a way to recognize something that occurred or that represents who the person is or how they have grown. When they have done well or made a shift in their thinking, point out specifically what you see. When you give constructive feedback about behavior, the focus is on the behavior. Conversely, when you acknowledge someone, the focus is on who he or she is and what he or she accomplishes. People need and appreciate acknowledgment. For example, you could say, "Tom, I want to acknowledge you. To me you are someone who keeps his word even when it is inconvenient or difficult."

> If you intend to develop your coaching skills, we advise working with a masterful coach.

Challenging

Challenging means pressing team members to stretch far beyond their self-imposed limits. A team coach collaboratively develops challenging coaching plans with team members that include specific goals and time frames. Together they review progress on a regular basis.

Listening for Context

Coaches learn how to listen without judgment to *everything*, whether spoken or not. We hear pauses, changes in tone, or emotions that don't match spoken words. Contextual listening is necessary to quickly understand an individual's frame of reference, wants, needs and concerns within the issues they bring to the coaching session. When a coach listens well, team members feel heard, respected and understood. In this way, the coach fosters an environment of trust that allows for rapid growth and problem solving. For example, a coach might say, "Let me tell you what I heard underneath all of this. Tell me if this rings true for you."

Preparing for Change

Changes in the business environment require greater self-responsibility for adopting new ways of communicating, behaving and achieving extraordinary results. Coaches condition people for change by first helping them understand the individual process of change. By understanding and appreciating how change impacts us, in time we will discover new possibilities for ways of being and acting. Thus, exploring possibilities leads to commitment, which leads to change. Your coaching helps people complete the cycle of change.

For example, a coach might ask "How would it look to you if you did x instead of y?" Or "What might break or what might happen if you continue as you have been?"

Creative Language

Creative language, including stories, metaphors, and models is an alternative to directive communication.

In telling stories we can create strong messages and make points without being directive. Team coaches use creative language to illustrate ideas and paint verbal pictures for team members. For example, we use many nautical metaphors in this book. We refer to a team project as the team's journey to a destination. We describe the role of a coach as being like a tactician's role on a sailing vessel. To become a masterful coach, begin collecting stories, metaphors and analogies to add to your repertoire.

Discovery Questioning

Discovery Questioning is a systematic process of asking sharply focused questions to help individuals discover how they are feeling and thinking. The team coach asks provocative questions that draw out personal understanding, or that evoke clarity, action, discovery, insight or commitment. When the coach is good at promoting discovery (that is, asking questions that create or enhance possibility, new learning or clearer vision), people discover powerful answers for themselves more quickly.

Informing

A skilled coach learns how to effectively sharpen the delivery of key information to create an environment where paradigm shifts and resultant action can occur. In this context, informing is a way of delivering a truthful message that is timely, personally relevant and succinct. For example, suppose you are coaching a leader who wants to delegate more responsibility. Over several weeks she reports on her frustrations and the inability of others to take responsibility. You may reply with: "The actions you are taking are not producing the results you want. It's time to look at other approaches."

> Straightforwardness without the rules of propriety becomes rudeness.
> —Confucius

Telling the Truth

Essentially, this skill entails saying what you intuit, feel or sense to be true about the situation. Telling the truth effectively first requires you to be deeply aware of your own agendas and to take responsibility for whatever you are feeling and thinking. From this position of self-awareness, you balance your sensitivity to others' feelings with your responsibility to tell the truth about what you see going on. For example, "Listen, John, you know it's my job to say everything that I sense and see, and this is one of those times . . . " Or, "Stephen, I have another perspective on that one. May I tell you what it looks like to me?"

Transformation

Transformation is more than a simple change in behavior; simple changes in behavior are only temporary. Transformation is a fundamental shift or reorientation of who you are, what you see and how you approach life. Masterful coaching causes personal evolution from the inside out and offers an invitation to make the leap to other possibilities rather than just changing someone's actions. The essential distinction is shifting who the person *is* versus what the person does. In this way, a team member can better effect a lasting change in behavior. A possible question to evoke a shift is: "Jim, who would you have to be in order to shift your leadership style from autocratic to collaborative?"

Confidentiality Is Key!

Confidentiality is the hallmark of the coaching profession. The coaching relationship is based on honesty, integrity, trust and confidentiality. All information that a client shares with a coach is held as confidential. This means that all information that a team member confides in you is not shared with anyone else without that person's expressed permission. It creates safety and trust and is the basis of the powerful alliance between team member and team coach. Refer to the Five Step Contracting Process in Chapter 5 for guidance in including terms of confidentiality in your agreement with the team.

DISTINGUISHING YOUR ROLE FROM OTHER ROLES

Before you start coaching your team, have a conversation with the team leader and/or the team sponsor about your role as team coach. The table below is intended to help you clarify your role and distinguish it from other roles on the team. It distinguishes between coach, consultant and team member, and team leader. These distinctions can at times seem blurred. For example, many consultants take a coach approach when applying their content expertise. However, we have found that when roles and responsibilities are not clearly defined and agreed upon, problems result. Take Table 1 as a guideline, first to have an internal dialogue with yourself in which you identify how you will work best with the team. In turn, take the outcome of that process to the contracting conversation you have with the team leader and team.

Role Comparisons

	Coaches	Consultants or Team Members	Team Leaders
Skills mastered	Have mastered coaching and relationship skills (i.e., listening, inquiring, reframing, truth-telling, creating distinctions, requesting)	Have mastered technical tasks, and in some cases process and relationship skills.	Have mastered personal effectiveness; empowering, managing and leading others towards business results. Have strategic business acumen.
Objectives	Focus on empowering the team to achieve results and integrate learning for future success and fulfillment. Balanced focus on people and task.	Focus on (co-)developing and/or implementing a developed solution for satisfying team goals.	Focus on the team's work and the successful completion of the project.

	Coaches	Consultants or Team Members	Team Leaders
Primary focus	Holds the vision that the organization has for itself. Helps the team align their actions to the organization and team vision of success.	Balance completing the work with nurturing relation-ships.	Have a vision for the direction of the team; inspire others by communicating regularly, and by modeling appropri-ate behaviors.
Solution develop-ment	Empower team leader and team members to design and execute their own solutions.	Provide solutions. Process consultants may involve the team more than content consultants do in formulating the solutions.	Aligns and manages solutions developed by team members with team charter and project goals.
Relation-ships	Keep an observant eye on the link between the team, its executive sponsors, and other teams to ensure a positive impact of the team's work.	Are aware of the overall context, however, they may or may not have the sponsors or other stakeholders involved in the team's work.	Are responsible for cultivating a powerful relation-ship between the team, its sponsors, and other teams.
Responsi-bility	Are responsible to the team process in a way that helps the team complete its work and individuals thrive in the experience.	Are accountable for a satisfactory completion of deliverable work product as agreed upon in the roles and responsibilities of the team.	Are responsible for the team process, achieving the team goals, and develop-ing team members.

Table 1: Role Comparisons

WHEN IS A COACH NOT A COACH?

In the flood of team activities, an enthusiastic coach can sometimes overstep his role. If this happens, this crossover of roles diminishes the impact of the coaching. The coach approach distinguishes and integrates the roles of all three—the coach, the team leader and team members—in a way that maximizes the effectiveness of all.

A mentor of ours was once coaching a team. She found herself agreeing to take meeting notes for her team. She was good at it, it filled a need on the team, and in doing so, she felt included in the work of the team. However, she became increasingly frustrated because her attempts to share observations or make coaching inquiries were met with little response by team members. Coaching sessions with the leader became less focused.

Her role as coach had blurred with the work of the team. We coached her to step back into the role of coach and away from the work of the team. To make this transition, she told the team leader what had happened: that she had stepped into a role as team member. She supported the team by having a team member take notes, and in time, her coaching became much more effective.

Here are some signs that indicate that the boundaries of your roles have become blurred:

- If you're the coach and you've started recording the minutes of the meeting, you're not coaching. Record keeping is the work of the team.
- If you're preparing communications to the organization about the team's proposed organizational changes, you're not coaching. Communication is the team's responsibility.
- If you are talking more than listening, then you're not coaching. You might be leading or directing the team.
- If you find yourself delegating and overseeing the tasks of the team, you are not coaching the team. You are managing it.

- If you are researching business information for the team's initiative, you are not coaching. You have joined the crew.
- If you need to be credited for the results the team has produced, you have lost sight of your role as coach. Credit for the results of the team is due to the team.
- If you are happy to be acknowledged for the impact that your coaching has on the team, then you're right on track.

CASE STORY: COACHING IN ACTION
The Situation

Jeanie, a team coach, had been asked to coach a team that had been given a yearlong charter to implement a new Enterprise Resource Planning system in a multi-billion dollar global corporation. The Executive Vice President (EVP) of manufacturing (the sponsor of the team) and the team leader agreed that they wanted to build a high impact team. The timelines were very aggressive and the project was complex. Despite the amount of work that was due, the EVP and Bill, the team leader, agreed that Jeanie's role was to help develop people and team cohesiveness. They understood that by developing people and their relationships, Jeanie would help the team create an environment in which a high impact team could emerge.

A team member was originally assigned to the role of executing the communications strategy. Half way through the project, budgetary constraints led the EVP to remove the communications lead from the project. A few months before the end of the project, team members became so absorbed in doing various tasks that they lost focus on delivering written communications to other parts of the organization that would be impacted by the change. The EVP realized that because the team had stopped disseminating information about its work, the rest of the organization was unaware of the impending change and wasn't preparing for the final implementation. The success of the project was at great risk—and no one was assigned to the task of creating the verbal bridge between the team and the larger organization. In frustration, the EVP demanded that Bill submit critical communications to the organization ASAP. In a subsequent meeting, Bill turned to Jeanie and assigned the responsibility of delivering written communications to her. "After all, coaching is about communications," Bill said. Jeanie was at a loss about what to do because the frantic team leader had asked her essentially to step outside her role as coach and do some of the team's work.

Observations

What might Jeanie be thinking about the dynamics of this situation?

"Why is Bill thinking I'm responsible for written communications—isn't my role clear? I may need to clarify my role again in the face of this crisis."

"Bill is reacting rather than responding to the EVP's demand. A coachable moment has presented itself for leader coaching."

"The team's charter was changed—the resource was lost for communications, breaking down the bridge between teams and the team sponsor, and a replacement approach wasn't implemented. This is an opportunity for the team leader to take this problem to the team to design a new approach or to work with the team sponsor to replace the lost resource."

In fact, all three ideas are true. First, the role of the coach became blurred. Second, Bill reacted to the demand. Third, the team's charter was changed and a new strategy wasn't implemented.

Coaching Strategies

Jeanie chose to address all three issues with a simple approach. The conversation started like this:

"We had agreed that I would focus on developing people and fostering an environment for peak performance and not be responsible for the team's work. I understand you're pressed to get this report out. Let's talk about how you want to respond to this problem while honoring our respective roles."

Our coaching to a coach in this situation is to step back with the team leader, to help him identify what leadership approach, team practice or perspective is missing and then make a commitment to action. In this situation, the team leader chose to present the problem to the team. Because Jeanie had started coaching, a collaborative environment was already underway to support solving problems such as this one. The team leader realized that he didn't have to have all the answers for solving the problem. Bill could take the issue to the team for resolution. A team member, whose work was nearly complete, volunteered to assume the responsibilities of the communications lead. He was keenly interested in developing his expertise in this area. The leader demonstrated a shift in beliefs: instead of owning all the problems and challenges, he empowered the team to solve the problem. Bill took a real-time opportunity to collaborate with the team. In this way, Bill integrated the coach approach and continued to foster an environment of high impact.

DISTINCTIONS

Distinctions separate two or more very similar words or concepts. Seeing fine distinctions enables individuals to take more discerning actions. Masterful coaching includes drawing distinctions as a tool for reframing one's perspective and responding more appropriately from this new perspective. The simplest example of this is the distinctions between managing and leading, which seems to confound many new, and even sometimes experienced managers. Tasks are managed; people are led.

Earlier in this chapter, we drew the distinction between coach, consultant, and team leader. In each chapter we will continue to draw distinctions for you to use in your coaching and leading.

INQUIRY

As you finish each chapter, you'll find an inquiry—a question to ask yourself to help you integrate the learning from the chapter and to stay focused on your values and your goals.

An inquiry helps an individual discover what she wants and why she wants it. Asking inquiry questions allows clients to go deeper inside themselves to clarify the real issues while staying focused on their values and goals. Inquiries can be action-oriented (How do you get what you want?), thought provoking (What's your thinking on that?), feeling (How is it affecting you?), and rhetorical (stating an observation as a question that doesn't have an answer when asked). For example, in a coaching session, we posed the inquiry, "What mindset do you want to take to work with you so that you can begin to enjoy your work?" We asked the client to ponder this question and not respond immediately. The client called us unexpectedly four weeks later and announced, "I've started enjoying my work."

From what you've read so far, what will be your biggest challenge in being an effective team coach and what strategy will you use to overcome that challenge?

CHAPTER 2

The Team Leader As Captain

Leadership is the art of mobilizing others to
want to struggle for shared aspirations.

—James M. Kouzes and Barry Posner
The Leadership Challenge

Team leaders are ultimately accountable to the organization for the team's results. Leaders are also responsible for the impact their behavior has on the team's culture and its performance. How, then, does a leader ensure that his or her impact on the team and the team's work is positive? This chapter addresses issues that are unique to leaders, on the understanding that coaches will "listen in."

Contrary to the idea that "leaders are born, not made," leadership can be learned by those who wish to learn it. As a leader, you can assess and intentionally optimize the impact you have on people and performance. You can understand how your leadership strategies are shaping the behavior and performance of others. If you study and implement the coaching strategies presented in this chapter, you will have identified and leveraged the leadership competencies that are more likely to have the desired results. Adopt the practices in this book, and you will have adopted the coach approach to peak performance.

THE LEADER'S IMPACT ON TEAM PERFORMANCE

Accomplished team leaders are conscious of their impact on their peers and their team members at all times. Successful team leaders intentionally behave in ways that demonstrate their values and commitment to peak performance. Because of the natural power hierarchy, whether they like it or not, the leader's behavior commonly becomes the norm for the team.

> What you do speaks so loud that I cannot hear what you say.
>
> —
>
> Ralph Waldo Emerson

During a corporate turnaround initiative, Jim, the newly hired CEO, noticed that members of the executive team constantly gossiped about each other. Jim guessed (correctly) that this was a common practice of the previous CEO. He saw this as a bad habit that inhibited people from taking responsibility for their work and their communications. Jim decided to put a stop to it. At a staff meeting, he said, "I have noticed that you are talking about your peers when they leave the room. While this may have been okay before, it's not okay any more. I want you to trust each other, and gossiping is one sure way of killing trust and responsibility." But the story isn't over.

After Jim relayed this story to us, he asked for shadow coaching during the next team meeting. We discussed Jim's objectives for the coaching and he stated he wanted to always tell the truth without judgment. During the next meeting we observed that he was also guilty of talking about people behind their backs. We provided him feedback in a way that modeled nonjudgmental truth-telling, saying, "Jim, we know you are committed to transforming this leadership team. Can we share an observation with you in the spirit of that commitment?" He looked at us curiously and nodded. "We noticed you were complaining about an executive on your team with other team members. Instead of complaining about that person, what request have you not made of him or what feedback have you not delivered?" Understanding his learning style, we knew he would take this direct feedback, reflect on it and see what behavioral change he needed to make. Over time, we observed that his communication became more constructive and timely for each of his direct reports and his peers. He didn't change in order to change others; he simply realized his behavior was ineffective. Previously, it had been okay to gossip and complain rather than take complaints to someone who could do something about a problem. In his effort to turn the company around, Jim saw that he had to change as an individual before he could lead change within the organization.

How would you assess the impact you are having on your team and team members? One possibility is to invite an objective observer in. You can hire a coach who utilizes some of the coaching strategies we discuss later in this chapter. Alternatively, you can investigate how you impact others by investigating the characteristics of the team that work well and don't work well. Take on this investigation for two weeks. Finally, ask yourself how the observed characteristics relate to the way you operate as a leader.

SHARED LEADERSHIP

The term "shared leadership" contrasts with the "command and control" style of leadership in which control and authority rests exclusively with those at the top of the organizational ladder. High impact teams share leadership. In other words, team members assume decision-making authority and responsibility for the team's results. By instilling the notion that every team member is responsible for the team's success, you develop leadership within the team.

The idea of shared leadership is based on mutual respect and caring for all team members. Intentionally modeling leadership competencies has the effect of distributing leadership throughout the team. Far from diminishing the leader's influence on the team, distributing responsibility throughout the team highlights the leader's significance while bringing out the best in others. In the traditional command and control model, the leader's trust of the abilities of others is low. Hence leaders *command* employees in what to do and then *control* how they do their work. Minimal effort is expended in utilizing the intelligence of the team to improve its culture and performance. In turn, creativity, willingness to take initiative, and active ownership for results by team members is suppressed.

Leading a high impact team, on the other hand, requires the leader to be much more competent at listening, and at constellating a wide variety of tasks and individual needs. It is far more difficult to motivate a talented group of people to complete a coordinated cluster of tasks well than it does to order someone to comply. Generation X and Y, for example, will not tolerate command and control leadership. They commit their time and expertise when there is a personal connection, and not merely because someone commands it. The benefits of practicing shared leadership include attracting and retaining the best talent.

Capable leaders find that coaching helps them implement a shared leadership approach while focusing the team's momentum on results. Since the team leader is still ultimately accountable for the team's results, the leader must manage the paradox between giving away responsibility and retaining accountability.

SKILLS OF SUCCESSFUL TEAM LEADERS

Many theories have been advanced about what it means to have the "right stuff" to be a great leader. Effective team leaders are proficient in the following three roles: Personal Master, Business Professional and Developer of People and Teams. They are committed to building the characteristics and skills required to meet the challenges of these three roles. Which of these skills is critical in leading your team to high impact status? Which of these skills and characteristics come naturally to you? Are you leveraging these talents?

Take a look at the following list of skills and characteristics of effective team leaders to set your own course of leadership development.

SKILLS AND CHARACTERISTICS OF MASTERFUL TEAM LEADERS
Personal Master

- **Self-Aware** of personal aptitudes, values, motivators, challenges and needs. Appreciates and applies own strengths and passions to manifest personal vision and mission.
- **Self-Manages** by demonstrating self-discipline, monitoring progress towards self-mastery and goals, and handling self well regardless of circumstances.
- **Demonstrates Integrity** by behaving consistently with beliefs and values. Assumes a high degree of personal responsibility and follows through on agreements and commitments.
- **Communicates Effectively.** Uses language that is respectful and free of bias, jargon, or judgment. Creates a culture in which timely, quality information flows smoothly. Listens fully to what others have to say, and encourages their truthful self-expression.
- Committed to **High Personal and Professional Standards** and challenges others to raise their standards. Is a strong positive example for others.
- Takes time to focus on **Personal and Professional Development**. Seeks truthful feedback to continually grow and develop as a leader. Tends to be curious and is driven to find ways to achieve full potential.

Business Professional

- Inspires a **Compelling Vision** and ensures that team members work towards the organization's mission and goals.
- **Manager of Results.** Collaboratively sets and achieves short- and long-term goals.

- **Gains Sponsorship.** Involves project sponsors and other key organizational leaders early and often in the creation of a team charter. Sets the expectations for sponsor participation.
- **Strategist.** Demonstrates business acumen in core business areas including profitability, customer service, and organizational planning. Balances qualitative and quantitative measures of success.
- **Transformational Leader.** Anticipates changes in customer and employee needs and changing market conditions. Responds by transforming business practices and organizational culture.
- **Provides Meaningful Rewards and Acknowledgment** for individual and team performance. Aligns rewards appropriately with what is meaningful to the individual.

Developer of People and Teams

- **Engenders Trust.** Exhibits openness, sincerity, reliability, and competence.
- **Fosters a Safe, Supportive Environment.** Demonstrates respect for team members' communication, work, and learning styles that creates opportunities for risk-taking and contributing in valuable ways.
- **Empowers.** Communicates what is expected for extraordinary performance, gives authority, and gets out of the way.
- **Builds High Impact Teams.** Institutes effective team practices, provides opportunities for team members to contribute to their fullest potential, and clears away interference to success.
- **Provides Support, Resources and Encouragement** for individuals and teams adopting new behaviors and actions, including those that involve risk-taking or those that elicit anxiety.

- **Values Ongoing Learning.** Helps individuals and teams to see what's ahead and to identify the learning, experiences, and actions they need in order to get to the next level.

A sea captain selects the destination and timing of the journey (Compelling Vision). The captain is concerned with his own emotional and physical well being; otherwise he won't be able to maintain composure under the pressure of changing weather and sea conditions (Personal Master). In conjunction with the officers, the captain determines the most effective utilization of the ship's resources and its personnel (Strategist). The captain must take into account all factors that would affect the ship and the voyage.

The Titanic sank because the Captain disregarded the safety of his ship and personnel in his attempt to set a cross-Atlantic speed record.

By way of contrast, Paul Cayard, captain of the notorious racing sailboat AmericaOne, was a developer of people. When he assembled his crew, he first assessed the requirements for each position (Strategist). After staffing the crew, he developed the team by first earning their respect through his own high standards, professional expertise and genuine caring (Personal Master).

Like Paul, every captain is responsible for developing the competencies of every crew member (Developer of People and Teams). Even in peacetime, every Navy ship has battle training, where the crew practices battle drills to develop their competencies.

BECOMING A MASTERFUL CAPTAIN

In the flurry of pressing activities, team leaders often find it difficult to take time out to consider how their leadership style impacts the team and how they might lead more effectively. A coach can work with you and the team to implement the Top 10 High Impact Team Practices (see Chapter 3). However, when leaders are not engaged in their own professional development, then their ineffectiveness may neutralize the work of the team coach. Since, you are reading this book, our assumption is you are committed to developing your team leader competencies.

You can develop on your own by reading books on leadership, working with a mentor in your organization, tapping into your peer network, attending workshops and utilizing the skills of a team coach. In the coach approach to professional development, you can work with a coach in a variety of ways to leverage and develop your own "right stuff." One-on-one coaching is the most effective approach. Coaching sessions can be conducted in person or by telephone. Combined with one-on-one coaching, we also suggest using assessment tools and shadow coaching.

One-on-One Coaching

The goal of coaching is to help you develop specific leadership competencies that will contribute to your ability to produce your desired business results. In private coaching sessions, you will receive nonjudgmental and truthful feedback that no one else may be willing or able to provide. You will discover new skills to address the real time issues you are facing.

A coaching agreement is most effective when it is designed to elicit both the leader's and the coach's best work. When you contract with a coach, your agreement will include the purpose and goals of the coaching, frequency of coaching sessions, the terms of confidentiality, and each person's role in the coaching relationship. Coaching can include pre-scheduled appointments, or coaching as needed. We call this "spot" or just-in-time coaching. Spot coaching is a ten-minute phone call during the week, a faxed letter, or an e-mail requesting coaching on a specific issue. In Chapter 5, we introduce the five-step contracting process for establishing an effective coaching agreement.

Qualified coaches establish a format for your coaching sessions. For example, in our coaching engagements we start coaching conversations by establishing the focus of the day's session. Using discovery questions and listening for context, we help leaders uncover other perspectives and alternative actions. After developing an action plan and clearing obstacles, the session comes to a close when the leader summarizes what actions they will be taking and what insights they've had in the conversation.

Coaching sessions will cover one or more of these topics:
- Accomplishments
- Current challenges, issues, or opportunities
- Future business interactions
- Business strategies
- Skill development

Using Assessment Tools

Assessment tools offer an excellent starting point for feedback, team coaching activities and regular coaching conversations. Assessments offer quantifiable information about a wide range of topics and behaviors and have a credible reputation in the corporate arena. What we find is that when we present the key competencies of a strong leader or a strong team, leaders who are committed to high performance want a means to know how they're doing and to track their progress.

Our objective in this section is to introduce you to several assessment tools that we have found valuable in our work with team leaders and teams. These assessments are intended to help people use their strengths more effectively in the workplace. Entire books have been written about these tools and how to use them. Our intent is to provide an overview of individual and team assessments so you can have a conversation with your coach. (The Appendix contains a resource list for the major assessment tools available.)

Personality and behavioral assessments, such as the Meyer's Briggs Type Indicator (MBTI) and the DISC, give you, the team and the coach insights into who is on the team. They illuminate the strengths and natural talents on the team, point out what talents are missing, and they serve to help the team to answer the question "how can we work best together?" With most of the teams we work with, we find that important team issues can be resolved through team coaching activities using assessments.

We were invited to work with a leadership team responsible for a one-year product development project. They wanted team members to take responsibility for solving problems rather than giving endless reasons for late work and product performance that didn't meet customer expectations. The team leader was frustrated and simply felt she had exhausted all her options. Their ultimate goal was to significantly raise the level of customer satisfaction and to deliver a product on time that they could be proud of. The High Impact Team Assessment and interviews with team members revealed that the leadership group did not get along with or trust each other. Hence, their ability to solve real business issues was impaired. After a team coaching activity with the DISC assessment, work-related diversity exercises, and follow-up coaching for four months, they reported on their progress. They now address their issues more frankly and collaborate to develop innovative solutions for moving forward. They have given up trying to change each other and are learning how to use their diversity to their advantage.

Whereas the DISC and MBTI assessments are self-scoring (people fill out a questionnaire about themselves) the 360 Degree Feedback Assessment gathers feedback from the leader's peers, subordinates, boss and customers (if appropriate). The 360 Degree Feedback Assessment can be the most comprehensive feedback tool for a leader. It provides straight feedback on the perceptions of others about the individual's behavior in their role. Coach and leader design a survey that specifically asks for feedback on the key competencies for the leader in the current role. With the feedback, the leader and coach design a development plan that leverages their strengths and helps them overcome their challenges.

Shadow Coaching

In shadow coaching, the coach and team leader agree on a meeting or time when the coach will observe the leader "from the shadows." You and the coach agree on what the coach is to observe and how and when you want to receive the feedback.

The benefits of shadow coaching are tremendous when leaders receive immediate feedback with specific examples about ways of behaving and their impact on people. Constructive feedback should address not only the ways you behaved that might not serve you well, but also what you do well. Shadow coaching enhances your one-on-one coaching, in which you relive events with only your perspective.

There are risks in shadow coaching. If the coaching relationship is new, and trust between you and the coach has not been established, you may not be ready to receive their direct feedback. In this early stage, it might also damage the coaching relationship. Another concern for many leaders is that team members will respect them less because they have a coach. Yet a leader is usually at greater risk of losing the team's respect if he is unwilling to accept feedback and adopt new behaviors.

Bob, a director at a Fortune 100 company, was assembling his department for a problem-solving workshop and asked his coach for shadow coaching. Bob was clear that the poor performance of one group was having an impact on the overall efficiency of the department. The workshop was designed to improve the overall efficiency of the department. Because of the cultural and gender diversity in his department Bob carefully crafted the format of the session.

He wanted shadow coaching on the effectiveness of his communication, his ability to engage participation, and his ability to empower them to take ownership of creatively solving the department's problems. In our pre-workshop coaching session, Bob strategized about the content of the workshop, and also his leadership development intentions. Before jumping into the content of the session, he clarified his vision for his own leadership and for the outcome of the meeting. He asked for feedback on how his behavior matched those two intentions.

In the feedback session after the workshop, we first asked Bob to share his perceptions of what worked and what didn't. He acknowledged that his teams collaborated on solving a very real business problem whereas in the past they would have pointed fingers, argued and not come to resolution. "It was so easy. I didn't have to control the meeting to get input." In analyzing what he did differently to produce this result, he described the approach many athletes use. First, he got clear on the desired outcome. He then visualized the process he wanted—natural leadership on his part and collaboration on the team's part. Plus, he was clear and inspiring when he described to the participants the outcome he wanted to create.

"I always just wrote and memorized the layout of my presentation, never clarifying what I wanted the interaction to look like or the outcome I wanted." We acknowledged him for his relaxed persona and that he allowed his sense of humor to complement his intelligence. He connected with his team on a personal level without pretense. Since that time, it has become Bob's practice to not only prepare content and clarify his leadership intent, but also to always remain connected personally with the team.

CASE STORY: FROM MANAGER TO LEADER
The Situation

Susan, a project manager with a technical background, is working for a highly successful Internet technology company. She has just been assigned to head up a team charged with developing and implementing a web-based software solution for a Fortune 500 company. The project is expected to last six months and brought her employer over $500,000—the largest sale in the company's two-year history.

She's excited about the project because it is technically advanced, high profile, and she's an expert in this area. She's also worried. This will be the largest team she's ever led; the project is technically challenging and its high profile makes mistakes very visible. The company is known for over-promising and under-delivering client projects.

Sales people regularly discuss schedules with clients that the development team can't meet. Since she's been with the company (only four months) she has been recognized for being an excellent project manager who delivers quality product in a relatively short period of time. In this project, she participated with the sales process to scope out the work and estimate schedules. Her boss has acknowledged her talent by delegating full responsibility for this project to her—something he previously would have handled himself.

Here's the catch: Susan is used to managing engineers. Now, she's being asked to lead a multi-disciplinary team of professionals from her organization and from its client company. Her personal style is very focused; this is a trait which many people experience as "too intense" or even "pushy." However, her style has not held her back in managing technical projects.

She calls her coach: "Help! I'm headed off to the first meeting and I'm stressed out. What do I do?"

Observations

What are some of the issues that might come up for Susan?

1. She might be concerned about how this project will impact her reputation and future in the company.
2. She might be concerned about the team's and the client's judgments about her professional ability to lead the team effectively.
3. She might be concerned about the technical talent she has on the team and whether or not they've got what it takes to get the work done.
4. She might be concerned about the promises made to the client and whether or not they can be met.
5. She may want to work out how she's going to kick off the project both internally and with the client.

> You don't have to control your thoughts, you just have to stop letting them control you.
>
> —
>
> Dan Millman

Coaching Strategies

Possible coaching strategies in this situation can include one or more of the following:

- Identify the issues that are most critical to focus on in her coaching session.
- Identify her vision of a successful conclusion to the project and what kind of leader she needs to be in order to realize the vision she's created.
- Briefly review the first phase of a team's development. In developing Susan's empathy, have her stand in the shoes of the team members on this new team: What must they be thinking? What might they want?
- Strategize about launching a high impact team (see Chapters 5 and 6).

Conclusion

Susan has a driving, task- and results-oriented style and is known for steamrolling. She hired us to coach her to lead more effectively; her organization would only continue to grow and grow. She wanted to learn how to responsibly delegate so that she could lead. Her commitment to use coaching to develop her leadership skills, and to add a team approach to the company's project management methodology, paid off handsomely. The company and its clients now trust Susan's team to complete projects on time and within budget—and it's not a struggle. She has been promoted twice and is now a Vice President.

Susan describes her experience this way: "I have put a management structure in place that supports the rapid growth of my team as well as the staggering number of projects we're executing (I started out managing three or four projects and we have 35 currently). I have open and authentic communication with my team, and have heard from team members that they've learned a lot from me about how to communicate with integrity. The CEO went out of his way to acknowledge my team for how well we implement projects while under pressure, across multiple internal groups and customers, with almost no conflict. I feel this is a direct result of some of the coaching I've done with my team on direct and constructive communication, keeping their eyes on the goals rather than on being right or making others look bad."

DISTINCTIONS
Managing v. Leading

To manage is to direct and control the tasks or people on a team. This is the natural approach for many technically oriented managers who have not developed leadership skills. To lead is to guide or influence; it involves setting direction and communicating what matters most. It enables people to create anew and challenge the status quo. In this chapter's case story, Susan learned the difference between managing the tasks on the project and leading the team towards their vision of high performance.

Control v. Power

Control is used to restrict, restrain or regulate something or someone. Power is the ability to make things happen through skill, influence, or authority. When one uses control the outcome is limiting, except in situations of real danger where it is beneficial. If one uses power in influencing and inspiring others, one doesn't need control over every step of a project.

If your thoughts are controlling you, you're probably controlling people.

Extrinsic v. Intrinsic Motivation

With extrinsic motivation, the reward is external to the activity and to the person. For example, offering trips and prizes for meeting sales quota competitions is extrinsic motivation. When used to motivate behavior, external rewards are a diminishing resource that ultimately drains the company's talent. Intrinsic motivation occurs when the work is its own reward. When they get to use their skills and talent, people spend their time doing what they enjoy doing. As a leader, your job is much easier if your team is intrinsically motivated.

INQUIRY

How do you want people to describe you as a leader?

How effective are you as a leader?

From the table of Skills of Successful Team Leaders, which skills will you develop?

CHAPTER 3

Charting Your Course:
The Crew As a High Impact Team

Men and women want to do a good job, and if they
are provided the proper environment, they will do so.

—Bill Hewlett
Co-founder, Hewlett-Packard

A High Impact Team (HIT) is defined as an energetic group of people that produces high quality, planned results in a defined period of time despite difficulties. HIT members are committed to achieving common goals using their diverse skills, personalities, and talents. Assuming both individual and collective accountability for the success of the team, they support one another in clearing away obstacles. Team members collaborate and enjoy working as a high impact team.

By contrast, a nominal team is a group of people having both mutual and individual accountability to produce stated results. You might infer, then, that a classic sales "team" is not really a team in that they predominantly have individual accountability and individual reward. How might you classify a group of people, from several departments of two companies, who have been brought together for a year in order to merge the two companies' functional, financial, and market aspects? Is it a team? If so, is it a high impact team? Maybe you would have to observe them to find out.

When you become familiar with what a high impact team truly is, what's missing on your team becomes apparent. The gap is clear and your work to close the gap can begin. Yvonne, a VP of a high tech company, realized that there were battlegrounds dividing her development group and the quality assurance (QA) group. Conversations led to internal arguments and blame. Problems reported by customers were met with "they should have" statements and finger pointing. Clearly this was not behavior that would promote the enjoyment of work or an innovative resolution for the customer.

> Peak Performance: To perform at your best, you have to set yourself apart from others' expectations of you.

With coaching, Yvonne learned that her behavior had the most impact on her team; she was completely willing to take responsibility for it. Furthermore, Yvonne recognized that she and Bill, the QA leader, had a pattern of blaming each other's teams. With this insight and commitment to resolve issues "from the top down," she scheduled a conversation with her peer to address their collective impact on the team. Both agreed to collaborate towards solutions and give up "being right" and making the other team wrong. Once they had this agreement in place, they independently communicated it to their teams. Reflecting on the process, Yvonne said, "It amazes me how simple it was to turn this around, and how much energy and frustration had been expended maneuvering around this conflict."

THE TOP 10 HIGH IMPACT TEAM PRACTICES

From all of our practical experience and research, we have distilled high impact team performance into top ten practices. HITs demonstrate high scores in each of these areas, although the process by which they achieve this level of team functioning is unique for each team.

When the team leader and team members intentionally commit themselves to strive for excellence as they define it, they make a crucial investment in their team's long-term success. At the beginning of each coaching engagement, we conduct interviews with the team leader and team members to assess how they believe they are doing as a team and what they perceive as working well or not working. With the HIT assessment (see page 78), you can analyze your team's gap between current reality and peak performance.

By no means do we rigorously insist on a pre-defined formula for developing the ten practices of high impact teams. Instead, we encourage teams to set their own target standards for each of the practices based on the team's charter and values. We share these Top 10 HIT Practices with our teams to help them assess their strengths, and opportunities for improvement. Then we collaborate with them to plan an appropriate course of action. These Top 10 practices have stood the test of time. We will elaborate on each in the following chapters.

IMPLEMENTING THE TOP 10 HIGH IMPACT TEAM PRACTICES WITH WORK GROUPS

True teams are very different than work groups. And yet, work groups can significantly raise their productivity, morale and work satisfaction by adopting the practices of high impact teams.

A work group is a collection of people gathered or structured together to work for an indefinite period of time. For example, a Customer Support Department is a work group—they report to the same manager and share systems, resources or technical expertise. Often though, work groups can experience pain stemming from the lack of common focus and commitment. On the other hand, a team that has a common focus, and leverages the sense of urgency that a time limit provides, can get more done in less time.

The Top 10 High Impact Team Practices

Practice	Description
1. Shared Purpose and Vision	• If you asked each of us why we are here as a team and what we're working towards, the answer would be the same and you can see it in our actions.
2. Shared Leadership	• We each take responsibility for the team being successful. Leadership is propagated throughout the team: all members operate with the same purpose and vision as the leader.
3. Measurable Performance Targets and Definable Goals	• We have agreed to specific, measurable, achievable, and time bound goals; they include both business and team development objectives. • We have established and we track measurable performance targets that move us towards our goals. • We regularly evaluate how we are working together as a high impact team.
4. Clear Roles and Responsibilities	• We each know not only the activities we are individually accountable for, but also what we are collectively responsible to produce. Each team member's role is clear. • We respect each person's role and openly discuss our expectations for the responsibilities of each role.
5. Active Sponsorship	• Our sponsors are involved and committed to our success, and support us in clearing away obstacles. • Our sponsors are proponents of our work and delegate the appropriate authority. • We have the resources we need to be successful: information, money, time, space, and talent.

The Top 10 High Impact Team Practices

Practice	Description
6. Effective Team Process	• We have a Working Agreement for our approach to our work and revise it when necessary.
	• We have practices for Effective Meetings, Integrating New Team Members, Decision Making, and Problem Solving.
	• We are competent at giving and receiving constructive feedback and coaching.
7. Enhanced Team Competency	• Our team acknowledges conflict and deals with it when it arises.
	• We have the flexibility to integrate change.
	• We are able to correct our course when off course, and adapt to changing conditions.
8. Synergistic Collaboration and Innovation	• Trust, accountability, and integrity are strong in our relationships. Communication and dialogue fosters action.
	• We collaborate to innovate new products or services and to solve problems when they arise.
	• We use both task, and task-free activities to infuse our team with creativity, celebration and renewal.
9. Meaningful Recognition and Rewards	• We are committed to each other's and the team's success. We acknowledge both individual and team achievements and personal development.
	• We recognize values-based performance in a meaningful way.
10. Quality Relationships with Stakeholders and Other Teams	• We coordinate our efforts with other stakeholders in a timely fashion.
	• We develop good relationships with other teams.
	• Our work is integrated with the company's overall business goals.

Table 2: The Top 10 High Impact Team Practices

We assert that a work group that embodies the practices of high impact teams transcends the ordinariness of everyday work to discover the enthusiasm and accomplishment that comes from being a part of a vital mission.

Whereas a team's journey is analogous to a cruise from California to Fiji, the journey of a work group is more similar to traveling on several around-the-world cruises. For example, the Customer Service Department might set the goal for the first leg of this year's around-the-world cruise as raising their technical competency. First, the leader would create his Vision. Next, he would share the Vision with the work group and they would define long- and short-term performance targets and goals, incorporating objectives the company has set for them.

For instance, this group might strive to solve 60% of all customer support calls on the first call. Using the High Impact Team Assessment that follows, work groups set a course that utilizes the strengths uncovered in the assessment, and addresses the opportunities for improvement. In this way, they not only accomplish meaningful business objectives, but they also raise their competency as a team for future challenges.

> Only use the assessment if you plan to address what is discovered. When follow-through is lacking, peoples' perceptions of how things are worsen.

THE HIGH IMPACT TEAM ASSESSMENT

As a living system composed of many human beings, a team needs to maintain a basic level of health in many different areas in order to function at its best. The HIT Assessment has been used in many companies to turn an average or less-than-average team into a high impact team. In a safe and non-judgmental way, the HIT Assessment objectively pinpoints areas of strength, gaps in performance, and areas for improvement. As a result, you and the team can design the most effective course of action for reaching high performance and accomplishing the team's objectives.

When we start working with a new team, we give the assessment to each team member. If time allows, we conduct one-on-one interviews by phone or in person with each team member.

Our objective is to hear first-hand any additional comments or perspectives a team member may have about an area of team functioning. Alternatively, we have team members complete the assessment on paper and submit it for anonymous compilation and follow-up discussion. We recommend that team leaders have an objective third party (a coach or Human Resources professional) administer the assessment, creating the opportunity for team members to provide truthful feedback.

We then coach the team leader to conduct a team meeting to discuss the results. The purpose of the meeting is to recognize team strengths and to identify the team's objectives for improvement. The value of the assessment isn't in the numerical results alone. Value comes from the feedback conversation, acknowledgment of strengths and follow-through on commitments made to each other.

The HIT Assessment has a variety of applications. As a benchmark, conduct the assessment at various points along the team's journey to highlight accomplishments, team strengths and next steps in the team's development. For teams that are new, the assessment creates a basis for generating team development objectives. In other words, if the team commits to being a high impact team, then it commits to having each of these ten practices present on the team. In this way, the assessment is educational. If a team has been together for a period of time or a team is experiencing problems, the assessment can be used barometrically to diagnose the source of its problems.

Conducting the assessment with your team will assist you in prescribing a course of action. Let's look at a team whose assessment results indicate they haven't become skillful at resolving conflict. You will discover that they are in the Weathering Storms phase described later, in Chapter 7. Potentially, one of your first activities to move them to Effective Sailing will be to help them become adept at managing their differences.

> By highlighting strengths and benchmarked improvements, you build team confidence and team esteem.

High Impact Team Assessment Form

Instructions: Indicate the extent to which you *agree or disagree* with each statement. Reflecting on your own experience working on this team, circle the appropriate rating point.

1 = Strongly Disagree
2 = Somewhat Disagree
3 = Neither Disagree nor Agree
4 = Somewhat Agree
5 = Strongly Agree

Practice Statement	**Rating**
1. If you asked each of us why we are here as a team and what we're working towards, the answer would be the same and you can see it in our actions.	1 2 3 4 5
2. Team members have a shared vision of team and organizational success.	1 2 3 4 5
3. We each take responsibility for the team being successful; all team members operate inside the same purpose and vision as the leader.	1 2 3 4 5
4. We have agreed to specific, measurable, achievable, and time bound goals; they include both business and team development objectives.	1 2 3 4 5
5. We have established and we track measurable performance targets that move us towards our goals.	1 2 3 4 5
6. We regularly evaluate how we are working together as a high impact team.	1 2 3 4 5
7. We each know not only the activities we are individually accountable for but also what we are collectively responsible to produce. Each team member's role is clear.	1 2 3 4 5 1 2 3 4 5
8. We respect each person's role and openly discuss our expectations for the responsibilities of each role.	1 2 3 4 5
9. Our sponsors are involved and committed to our success, and support us in clearing away obstacles.	1 2 3 4 5

Practice Statement	Rating

10. Our sponsors are proponents of our work and delegate the appropriate authority. — 1 2 3 4 5

11. We have the resources we need to be successful: information, money, time, space, and talent. — 1 2 3 4 5

12. We have a Working Agreement for our approach to our work and revise it when necessary. — 1 2 3 4 5

13. We have practices for Effective Meetings, Integrating New Team Members, Decision Making, and Problem Solving. — 1 2 3 4 5

14. We regularly assess how we are working together towards our goals and are competent at giving and receiving feedback and coaching. — 1 2 3 4 5

15. Our team acknowledges conflict and deals with it when it arises. — 1 2 3 4 5

16. We have the flexibility to integrate change. — 1 2 3 4 5

17. We are able to correct our course when off course and adapt to changing conditions. — 1 2 3 4 5

18. Trust, accountability, and integrity are strong in our relationships. Communication and dialogue produces action. — 1 2 3 4 5

19. We collaborate to innovate new products or services and to solve problems when they arise. — 1 2 3 4 5

20. We use both task, and task-free activities to infuse our team with creativity, celebration and renewal. — 1 2 3 4 5

21. We are committed to each other's and the team's success. We acknowledge both individual and team achievements and personal development. — 1 2 3 4 5

22. We recognize values-based performance in a meaningful way. — 1 2 3 4 5

23. We coordinate our efforts with other stakeholders in a timely fashion. — 1 2 3 4 5

24. Our work is integrated with the company's overall business goals. — 1 2 3 4 5

Scoring the High Impact Team Assessment

Now that you have collected the team's assessments, collate their responses as follows. Create two charts: one to analyze the team's ratings for each statement (see Table 3 below), and a second chart to analyze the team's ratings for each practice (see Table 4 below).

1. **For Each Statement** (using Table 3: Analysis of Statement Responses as an example):

    i.   Note the lowest and highest scores in the Ratings Range columns.

    ii. Calculate the average of the ratings from all respondents.

    iii. Calculate the percentage of response for each rating.

    iv. Calculate the standard deviation of the ratings from all respondents.

2. **For Each Practice** (using Table 4 as an example):

    i.   Calculate the average for all of the statements associated with that practice.

    ii. Calculate the Gap by subtracting the average score from a score of 5.

Sample Analysis of Statement Responses

Statements	Ratings Range		Avg Score	Ratings Spread % of Respondents					Std Dev
	Lowest	Highest		5	4	3	2	1	

Top 10 High Impact Team Practices

1. Shared Purpose and Vision

1	3	5	4.00	9%	82%	9%	0%	0%	0.447
2	2	5	3.91	9%	82%	0%	9%	0%	0.701

2. Shared Leadership

3	2	5	3.73	27%	36%	18%	18%	0%	1.104

3. Measurable Performance Targets and Definable Goals

4	2	4	2.64	0%	9%	45%	45%	0%	0.674
5	2	4	2.36	0%	9%	18%	73%	0%	0.674
6	2	5	3.45	9%	45%	27%	18%	0%	0.934

4. Clear Roles and Responsibilities

7	2	4	3.27	0%	45%	36%	18%	0%	0.786
8	3	5	4.27	36%	55%	9%	0%	0%	0.647

5. Active Sponsorship

9	2	5	3.64	9%	55%	27%	9%	0%	0.809
10	2	5	3.82	18%	55%	18%	9%	0%	0.874
11	2	5	3.55	9%	64%	0%	27%	0%	1.036

6. Effective Team Process

12	1	4	2.18	0%	9%	27%	36%	27%	0.982
13	1	4	2.45	0%	9%	36%	45%	9%	0.820
14	2	4	2.73	0%	18%	36%	45%	0%	0.786

7. Enhanced Team Competency

15	2	5	3.45	18%	36%	18%	27%	0%	1.128
16	3	5	4.36	55%	27%	18%	0%	0%	0.809
17	3	5	4.27	36%	55%	9%	0%	0%	0.647

8. Synergistic Collaboration and Innovation

18	2	4	3.09	0%	27%	55%	18%	0%	0.701
19	3	5	3.91	9%	73%	18%	0%	0%	0.539
20	3	5	3.64	9%	45%	45%	0%	0%	0.674

9. Meaningful Recognition and Rewards

21	2	5	3.64	18%	45%	18%	18%	0%	1.027
22	3	5	4.27	36%	55%	9%	0%	0%	0.647

10. Quality Relationships with Stakeholders and Other Teams

23	1	4	2.91	0%	36%	27%	27%	9%	1.044
24	4	5	4.27	27%	73%	0%	0%	0%	0.467

Table 3: Analysis of Statement Responses

Sample Analysis of Practice Responses

Top 10 High Impact Team Practices	Avg Score	Gap Score
1. Shared Purpose and Vision	3.95	1.05
2. Shared Leadership	3.73	1.27
3. Measurable Performance Targets and Definable Goals	2.82	2.18
4. Clear Roles and Responsibilities	3.77	1.23
5. Active Sponsorship	3.67	1.33
6. Effective Team Process	2.45	2.55
7. Enhanced Team Competency	4.03	0.97
8. Synergistic Collaboration and Innovation	3.55	1.45
9. Meaningful Recognition and Rewards	3.95	1.05
10. Quality Relationships with Stakeholders and Other Teams	3.59	1.41

Table 4: Analysis of Practice Responses

If you want to have the results of the assessment calculated for you, visit www.HighImpactTeams.com. The assessment results will be calculated for your team and e-mailed to you. We also help you identify your team's strengths, opportunities for improvement and recommended strategies for raising team performance.

MAKING SENSE OF ASSESSMENT RESULTS

Once you have completed calculating the results of the High Impact Team Assessment, you will want to make sense of the data. Having made sense of the data, you will be equipped to provide meaningful feedback to the team and to develop appropriate strategies for raising the level of team performance.

Look for Strengths

Not only do we want to acknowledge the team for their strengths but we also want to build on those strengths to:

- Enhance team esteem
- Raise other team competencies

- Focus team energies on important business objectives

Significant strengths are defined as those statements or practices where:

1. The Average Score is high relative to the other scores and more than 75% of the respondents rate this statement 4 or higher.
2. The Gap Score is low.
3. The Standard Deviation is relatively low.
4. At least 75% of the respondents rate this statement 4 or above.

Color-code these statements in your chart green.

Look at Table 3. You'll see that Statements 1 and 2 are clear strengths for this team. The numbers are taken from a real-life team that had a very clear vision for the company.

Look for an Absence of Clear Agreement

No clear agreement is a cautionary indicator for further investigation. In terms of ratings on the Assessment, you'll see a wide range of responses. No clear agreement can mean that the practice is misunderstood, that team members' perception of the competency differs, or that this topic isn't openly discussed and may in fact be avoided.

No Clear Agreement practices are identified as such when:

1. The Standard Deviation is relatively high.
2. Between 40% and 75% of the respondents rank the statement 4 or higher.

Color-code these statements in your chart yellow.

By default, most of us will look at what's not working and attempt to fix that first. In truth, it's more effective to look for those areas where performance is close to high impact and work there to achieve easy wins and immediate additional team esteem.

Look at the leadership team's responses in Table 3. They colored Statement 7 yellow and Statement 8 green. The team agrees strongly that they respect each other's roles (Statement 8), but they do not agree that their roles are clear (Statement 7). In this team, we saw this as an opportunity for a quick win: an area where we could use a team's strength to raise their competency in another team practice.

Look for Practices That Have the Greatest Opportunities for Improvement

The remaining statements point to practices the team has not yet developed. Possible reasons include them not having reached that phase in their journey, or not realizing they needed that practice. As you highlight these statements, consider how you will use your team's existing strengths to turn undeveloped practices into strengths.

Practices with the greatest opportunities for improvement are identified as such when:

1. The Average Score is relatively low.
2. Less than 40% of the respondents rank the statement 4 or higher.
3. The Standard Deviation is relatively low.

Color-code these statements in your chart red.

Matching the Results with the Team's Journey

Before you jump into action with this data, stop. This data alone will not give you a meaningful course of action. To co-create coaching objectives with your team, consider the data, the characteristics of each team development phase, and where the team is relative to meeting their business objectives. In the next and subsequent chapters, you will gain a deeper understanding of the phases of team development and how to develop the Top 10 HIT Practices. Also, you'll find in Table 5: Coaching Strategies for High Impact Teams, a matrix of strategies for developing a high impact team.

Guidelines for Providing Feedback

Prepare yourself for providing feedback to the team on their assessment results by:

- Completing the charts and analyzing the data
- Understanding the team's business objectives and where they are on their work plan
- Understanding the Top 10 HIT Practices
- Understanding the Phases of Team Development (See Chapters 4–9)

Here is a sample agenda for a feedback session. Use your creativity to design an agenda that matches your style and the team's style. Use the guidelines for holding effective meetings found in Chapter 6. If you want to provide a handout for the team, we recommend only a high-level review of the Assessments that does not include any details.

I. **Introduction:** The leader kicks off the meeting by discussing the purpose of the meeting, the meeting agenda, and the intended outcomes.

II. **An Overview of the Top 10 HIT Practices and the Phases of Team Development:** To set the context, describe the Top 10 HIT Practices and the phases of a team's development. When a team listens to what's possible, team members will be more open and discerning in receiving feedback on the team's current state.

III. **Provide the Feedback:** Using clean language and specific examples, work your way through the results of the team's assessment. Clean language involves keeping your own agenda out of your communication, preserving an open, neutral space without judgments and preconceptions. This approach creates openings for meaningful and safe discussion regarding the feedback.

> "Clean" language is devoid of judgments and assumptions. Clean language fosters the opportunity in others to make their own discoveries.

a. **Headline the Team Strengths:** Acknowledge the team for those practices that they demonstrate well. Don't skimp on acknowledgment.

b. **Discuss Areas of No Agreement:** The most common source of poor team performance stems from differing values, conflicts of ideology, and relationship dissonance. It is, therefore, critical to use clean language when discussing the areas of No Agreement. A skillful coach or leader is needed to guide this discussion in order to preserve the trust on the team while moving the team forward and resolving these issues.

c. **Present Opportunities for Greatest Improvement:** Describe those practices where the most improvement is available.

IV. **Co-create the Objectives for Coaching:** Teams that collaborate to set their own developmental objectives are more likely to be committed to the process.

a. **Discussion on Insights:** Give the team an opportunity to reflect on what they've heard. You might ask a question similar to: "Based on what you've heard so far, what are your thoughts?" Discuss their insights as a group.

b. **Creation of Objectives:** Now you're ready to transform the data into meaningful coaching strategies. The team has heard about the characteristics of a high impact team, and they now have an appreciation of their team's current state. When you sense the team is nearing clarity, focus the discussion on setting objectives. You might ask a question similar to: "In order to be effective as a team, what are the three critical elements you need next?"

c. **Specify the Objectives:** In this session or a subsequent meeting, spend time clarifying the objectives:

who is responsible, how will success be measured, who needs to be included, and when will they meet this objective.

V. **Recap the Outcomes of the Meeting:** Invite each person who is taking away an action to recap their accountability. Invite all participants to recap the value they are taking away from the feedback session.

VI. **Close the Meeting:** The leader provides closing remarks acknowledging the team for their work and participation, and for the objectives they have set for themselves.

COACHING STRATEGIES THAT MATCH THE TOP 10 HIT PRACTICES

Your team has defined its coaching objectives. Congratulations! It is now time to develop a plan to meet the team's desired level of high impact. Table 5 is a guide to selecting strategies and activities to develop each Top 10 HIT Practice. The art of navigating a team to high impact involves matching the right activities with the right timing. In other words, your ability to use the recommended strategies artfully depends on your sensitivity to the dynamics present in the team and your ability to envision the team's next appropriate destination. Go through the table and list potential activities without trying to organize them.

Coaching Strategies for High Impact Teams

Top 10 High Impact Team Practices	Developmental Coaching Strategies	Team Activities	Phases where Development of Practice is Critical
1. Shared Purpose and Vision	a) Identify Leader's vision for success b) Clarify team purpose c) Align team goals and task with organization's vision and purpose d) Match team outcomes with customer needs	a) One-on-one Leadership Coaching b) Completing Shared Purpose and Vision Activity c) Performing 5-Step Contracting Process	Preparing to Set Sail

Top 10 High Impact Team Practices	Developmental Coaching Strategies	Team Activities	Phases where Development of Practice is Critical
2. Shared Leadership	a) Identify required competencies b) Develop a clear set of working agreements c) Define agreement on how team will interact to achieve objectives	a) Performing 5-Step Contracting Process b) Anchoring	Preparing to Set Sail Setting Sail
3. Measurable Performance Targets and Definable Goals	a) Establish team goals for short & long-term accomplishment b) Define measurement performance process c) Involve stakeholders in the process d) Evaluate how team is working together	a) Setting performance targets b) Reviewing performance targets regularly	Setting Sail Effective Sailing
4. Clear Roles and Responsibilities	a) Identify talents and contributions critical to meeting objectives b) Support team leader in understanding individual work styles c) Support team members in understanding each other's contribution d) Foster responsibility and accountability	a) Conducting behavioral and style assessments to match natural talents to role needs b) Completing roles and responsibilities template (below)	Setting Sail
5. Active Sponsorship	a) Establish and monitor resources b) Strengthen relation-ships with Sponsors c) Manage team image within the organization	a) Describing and developing plans for garnering sponsorship b) Presenting the team storyboard (below)	Preparing to Set Sail Effective Sailing Arriving
6. Effective Team Process	a) Focus team energy where it is most beneficial b) Define practices for decision making & problem solving c) Develop processes for holding effective meetings d) Recapping	a) Ice-breaking b) Using red-light, green light model (below) c) Defining on-boarding processes	Setting Sail Weathering Storms Effective Sailing

Top 10 High Impact Team Practices	Developmental Coaching Strategies	Team Activities	Phases where Development of Practice is Critical
7. Enhanced Team Competency	a) Commit to address and resolve conflict b) Use talent of the whole team to solve problems c) Adjust and correct course d) Integrate change	a) Creating team winning opportunities b) Assessing meaning of change c) Performing 360 Degree Feedback (below) d) Utilizing Watchtower strategic assessment (below)	Weathering Storms Effective Sailing Arriving
8. Synergistic Collaboration and Innovation	a) Foster a safe environment b) Set ground rules c) Build on one another's creativity d) Foster greater levels of trust within the team	a) Developing communication skills b) Storyboarding (below) c) Uncovering and managing differences d) Idea Mapping (below)	Setting Sail Weathering Storms Effective Sailing
9. Meaningful Recognition and Rewards	a) Celebrate milestones & accomplishments b) Renew commitment of team members for team success c) Sustain momentum d) Ensure team members take personal time needed to refresh e) Give attention to meaningful moments in the team's life	a) Creating opportunities for renewal b) Offering one-to-one coaching c) Scheduling regular team outings d) Gathering the learning e) Completing the journey	Effective Sailing Arriving
10. Quality Relationships with Stakeholders and Other Teams	a) Identifying interdependencies between teams b) Connect with other teams c) Foster greater levels of trust and cooperation within the organization	a) Building strategies for communicating change and progress b) Presenting the team storyboard c) Demonstrate accomplishments to organization	Effective Sailing

Table 5: Coaching Strategies for High Impact Teams

CASE STORY:
A HIGH IMPACT TEAM IN THE MAKING

Harry, a leader of a regional consulting team in a global multi-billion dollar consulting firm, called us to find out more about Team Coaching and if it could help him. This leader was intent on developing a high impact team. He had a team of 12 professionals and was responsible for developing their technical expertise and leadership skills. Harry was feeling that although his team met in person occasionally and conducted effective meetings, they were missing the opportunity to experience the benefits of being on a *real* team. "We're narrowly focused on client results, which I like," he told us. "But there's no energy expended on developing team cohesion. If we had synergy and connection, the work would be much more enjoyable. We'd probably reduce burnout, and my guess is that we would be providing even better service to our clients."

In the initial contracting conversation, we first helped Harry clarify and articulate his vision for the team. To identify the gap between where the team is now and his vision, we next asked him about the current team performance. Once the gap was clear, we asked the simple question: What are your three objectives for the coaching? He replied:

1. Develop the leadership talents of each team member.
2. Inspire the team to work towards becoming a high impact team.
3. Enhance team productivity in a workplace with constant change and chaos.

Our initial agreement with the team, which we called *The 13-Session Journey,* was to assist the team in setting its own objectives, and then to conduct 13 two-hour teleconference coaching sessions to meet the team's and Harry's objectives.

Our first meeting with the team was brief. Harry introduced coaching, shared his purpose for inviting us in to work with the

> A gap exists when there is disparity between the current state and a future desired state. Create a gap. Use the natural tension that exists in the gap to move forward.

team, and asked for the team's participation in the process. We briefly described our background and provided an overview of the Top 10 High Impact Team Practices and the High Impact Team Assessment. Before our second team meeting, we conducted individual phone interviews with all team members. In evaluating scores and distribution, we found that there was little, if any, agreement on the statements. For example, some team members said there was a team purpose and vision, while others said there wasn't. Some team members said there was a process for dealing with disagreements, while others said there wasn't or that conflict was avoided. And so on down the list of statements.

In the feedback session, we reported the team's strengths: Clear Roles & Responsibilities and Enhanced Team Competency. The scores were high and the responses were aligned. Next we reported those practices where the team's average was lowest and where there was agreement: Synergistic Collaboration and Innovation, Shared Leadership, and Active Sponsorship. Harry's team was not at all surprised that their perceptions weren't aligned on 50% of high impact team practices. With this discussion behind us, it was time to empower the team to set its own objectives.

"Given the data and information about critical factors for success, where do you want to focus your energies over the next three months? What are your top three objectives for the coaching?" we asked them.

They set their objectives:
- Establish a shared purpose and vision
- Develop our individual leadership skills (Shared Leadership)
- Raise the level of trust on the team (a critical component of Synergistic Collaboration and Innovation)

We were then able to recommend topics for our monthly coaching sessions. Because they were involved in analyzing their team's

> A strong leader makes decisions. Whether they are right or wrong, they get made, and they are clear. A weak executive dilly-dallies and gives false signals, leaving subordinates to charge off in different directions.

performance and selecting objectives, they were committed to and successful in meeting their goals. Harry never dictated to the team what they were to do; he simply shared his vision and availed them of the coaching process. Harry was delighted that their objectives matched his and that the team was excited about the opportunity to work with a coach.

DISTINCTIONS
Mastery v. Competency v. Knowledge

Knowledge is information about a topic; it does not generally include experience. Competency is having the ability and skill to accomplish what is required, while mastery is having thorough or exceptional knowledge and skill. While competence is necessary to get what's needed done, mastery enables one to synthesize, innovate, and add to the subject.

This is an important distinction when selecting team members. You will want to assess where team members are on the continuum from knowledge to competence to mastery, and select team members with the skill appropriate to your time frame and goals. Be sure to consider how each team member's abilities complement the others.

Commitment v. Compliance

Commitment exists when observable action or change occurs that demonstrates commitment. It is an active, involved state. Compliance is a submissive state of acquiescing to a request or demand. If you are committed, you will be in action. Compliance can be accepted on nominal teams, but it is uncommon on high impact teams.

INQUIRY

How will you create an environment in which people can tell the truth about what's going on with the team?

PART II

PREPARING FOR A HIGH IMPACT JOURNEY

*I am always doing that which I
cannot do, in order that I may
learn how to do it.*

—Pablo Picasso

CHAPTER 4

Clarifying the Phases of Team Development

The future is not something we enter. The future we create.

—Leonard I. Sweet

Teams progress naturally through relatively predictable phases of development. Although each phase of performance shares common characteristics, each team's experience of each phase and of the journey is unique. Our intent in describing the journey is to help you understand these natural phases so that you can provide your team with a context in which to view its experience. When team members understand that what they are experiencing is a natural phase in their team's unfolding success, they find it easier to weather inevitable storms and setbacks and to take advantage of great conditions. By focusing the team's effort on finding ways to develop high impact competencies and high impact team practices, you can accelerate its progress toward high performance.

At the end of our description of each phase, we will recommend structured activities that help your team accelerate successfully through that phase. The activities guide teams through productive work sessions that result in well-defined actions. However, the activities alone will not leverage learning into changed behavior. Ongoing coaching provides the support to transform these new behaviors into regular practices. Continue to use Table 3 to develop your team.

THE PHASES OF TEAM DEVELOPMENT
Preparing to Set Sail and Setting Sail

In these first two phases, team members become acquainted with each other, establish ground rules and begin to establish working agreements. At this point, individuals may be concerned about whether they will fit in as members of the team and how they will make a significant contribution. Exchanges between team members are generally polite and guarded, and members may be reluctant to take risks and share their ideas. Team members generally defer most decisions and direction to the team leader.

As the team comes together, the team leader contracts with the coach and then with the team members about the team's purpose, objectives and tasks. At the start, the individual team members are watching to see how the agreements work in action. Will the team leader honor the contract? How will the team dynamics be manifested? Team members often ask themselves the following questions during this phase:

- Why am I here?
- Do I want to be a member of this team?
- Will others value my contribution?
- How much work is required?
- What are we supposed to accomplish and by when?

In this phase, it is critical for team members to find satisfying answers to these questions. When they do they will be ready to progress to the next phase.

Activities that assist the team in developing the critical practices for this phase include those that clarify the team's purpose and vision, set performance targets, define roles and responsibilities, and create a working agreement. Early wins in these activities generate confidence and the context for ongoing success. Our experience confirms that teams who get to high performance experience success early on, rather than waiting months to hit team milestones. We also find that in the next phase, Weathering Storms, these teams are more willing to be in healthy conflict.

Weathering Storms

It does not take long before teams begin to struggle with issues of power and influence. Weathering storms is a crucial time for the team leader and the coach to reinforce the notion that conflict can contribute to the team's ultimate success—as long as the team agrees to resolve its conflicts in healthy ways. More conflicts are likely to arise at this phase because members are unfamiliar with each other's styles. If the team manages its differences productively at this stage, it will carry the associated team skills into every phase that follows.

During this phase, frustration may also develop as team members struggle to find ways to work together. Confusion and disagreement about how to achieve team goals may play out in the creation of cliques, testing established working agreements, and resisting team activities. If a team loses headway for an extended period of time, it will fail to generate the momentum needed for later stages of the journey. Work will then be a struggle and the expense of effort will take its toll on the team.

Team members often ask themselves the following questions during this stage:

- Who has influence on this team?
- Can we work together to achieve our goals?
- What kind of behavior is acceptable on this team?
- What's not acceptable?
- What is my status on the team?

As it begins to weather storms, the team can add to the momentum it gained in the first phase. For example, although the team created a purpose and vision, it may still need to change the working agreements. By using activities and coaching that help team members clarify and reach agreement on the issues that separate them, you can help the team reduce the time it spends in storms. Critical practices to develop during this phase include Effective Team Process, Enhanced Team Competency, Synergistic Collaboration and Innovation.

Effective Sailing

This phase of team development is an outgrowth of the team's mastery of the previous phases of development. Teams reach full speed in this stage as they enter a period of smooth sailing. Meetings happen regularly, assignments are given and agreements are kept. Communication flows smoothly. Team members are proud and feel that they are included in the group's progress.

During this phase team members build on one another's creativity and are able to accomplish more together than the sum of individuals could alone. They will test their problem-solving and decision-making skills. They are aware of behaviors that build or undermine trust. As a leader or coach, your ability to help the team develop skills for integrating change, increasing creative thinking, nurturing team collaboration, and fostering an environment of trust will enable the team to sail effectively. The result is that members continue to build confidence and team esteem as they work together. Driven by the need to be productive, team members learn to interact constructively. It is essential for the team's continued progress that they not become complacent, but continue to enhance their team skills.

As team members strive to develop effective ways of working together and delivering results, they tend to focus on issues inside the team. However, it is important to maintain and even build relationships with other teams within the larger organization at the same time. Provide activities and feedback to ensure that a team develops these processes and their team skills quickly and efficiently.

Team members often ask themselves the following questions during this stage:

- How can we maintain accountability for results?
- What are the norms of acceptable behavior on this team?
- How do we use the talent of the whole team to solve problems?
- How do we sustain our momentum?
- How can we improve?
- What have we learned?

During this phase, teams continue to build on Shared Leadership, Measurable Performance Targets and Definable Goals, Active Sponsorship and Effective Team Process. It is now critical to develop the practices of Meaningful Recognition and Rewards, and Quality Relationships with Stakeholders and Other Teams. Strengthening relationships with sponsors for ongoing support to the destination must occur at this time. Employ task-free activities that infuse creativity and reenergize the team. Celebrating milestone accomplishments gives teams not only needed recognition, but also a break from the intensity of the work for needed renewal.

Arriving at the Destination

High impact teams work together for a defined period of time. At the end of that time, team members disband to form new teams or pursue individual assignments. Thus, in the final phase, most of the team's conflicts have passed and they need only to navigate their way into port—tying up loose ends, presenting results and declaring completion.

Finishing their task and disbanding the team is a significant event for all the team members. Individuals need to present the work to demonstrate its quality, nature, and its contribution to the larger organization. Presentation may also gain them visibility from others in the organization or with clients. Individuals will want to gather their newfound wisdom of working as a high impact team. Collection of this wisdom enables the individual and the organization to develop and sustain peak performance. Individuals also need to complete their journey with the team on an emotional level.

Team members ask themselves:

- What's next?
- What have I learned?
- What do I want to do differently on my next assignment?
- Were we successful?
- Will the company acknowledge our success?

As the team approaches port, activities for presenting the work, gathering the learning, and acknowledging team members for their contribution will be meaningful.

THE THREE Cs: CONFLICT, CHANGE AND COURSE CORRECTION

Although the phases of a team's journey to high impact appears linear, the truth is that teams experience ups and downs. No matter where a team is in its development, its team members need to have three skills if the team is to keep itself on a steady course. We call these three key skills the Three Cs. Teams must learn to apply the skills of managing *conflict,* integrating *change* and making *course corrections.* New circumstances may provoke a loss of headway and push the team back to an earlier developmental phase:

- Entry of new members or exit of existing team members
- Loss or availability of new information or resources
- Lost momentum due to ineffective team functioning
- Assignment of new team goals or projects by the organization

Mastery of the Three Cs is what distinguishes a high impact team from a nominal team. A high impact team has troubles and storms, but it overcomes them and moves on. They enjoy the work, grow in the process, and produce amazing results. Nominal teams might get the work done but be very late, work below their quality standards, and experience so much stress and burnout that team members end up feeling pessimistic and cynical about working with other teams in the future.

When you help your team members master the skills of conflict resolution, change integration and course correction, you empower them to succeed in the current project and to bring these vital capabilities into any team they work with in the future.

The First C: Resolving Conflict

By "conflict," we mean that people have different approaches, styles and opinions about the team's work and its members, and that they will feel strongly about the correctness of their points of view. In itself, conflict is neither good nor bad. It is a natural consequence of having a group of human beings working together. If there were no conflict, you'd have to check the pulse of every person on the team. Conflict has a bad connotation because people associate it with anger, argument, and other unpleasantness. Ironically, teams that consciously develop skills for identifying and resolving conflict actually experience fewer unpleasant forms of conflict than do teams in which conflict is considered a "bad" thing and is never mentioned. Teams with this emotional maturity have prepared themselves to handle conflict throughout the life of the team.

The coaching approaches that help teams learn to resolve conflict are:

1. Foster a safe environment in which people can express their differing points of view by setting the context, setting ground rules, and gaining agreement to resolve the conflict.
2. Validate the normalcy of conflict.
3. Develop a team process for conflict resolution.
4. Help team members integrate new way of being or install a new structure.

Team development is not linear— with good 3C skills teams progress in an upward expansive spiral after temporary setbacks.

The Second C: Integrating Change

Everyone knows that change is inevitable. However, few teams intentionally develop skills to rapidly assess the meaning of a particular change and to integrate that change into their continued effective functioning. A change can be something as minor as meeting in a different venue or as major as learning that the company is about to be acquired or that a team member is seriously ill. When team members know that they can manage whatever change comes their way, they approach their tasks with more enthusiasm, creativity and innovation. The key coaching skills for teaching teams to integrate change are:

1. Develop communication skills and trust so that differing points of views and possibilities can be openly addressed.
2. Identify the changes the team is facing; clarify which ones they have control over and which changes they need to adapt to or accept.
3. Help the team understand how individuals process change and how to coach others through change.
4. Develop a communications strategy for communicating change and progress to stakeholders.

The Third C: Staying On Course

Anyone who has driven a car knows that driving the car in a straight line requires the driver to make constant small adjustments with the steering wheel, accelerator and the brake. Similarly, when navigating the journey of a team, there is no such thing as a perfectly straight course. Conflicts and changes of varying magnitude arise. Sometimes these changes accumulate to the point that teams need to revisit their original vision and working agreements to see if they need to make fundamental adjustments. New members coming on board with new ideas or new information can impact the team's course positively or negatively.

> Every conflict is one between different angles of vision, illuminating the same truth.
>
> — Mahatma Gandhi

Even without intense conflict or extreme change, teams will tend to drift off course, or lose headway. These little drifts happen to all teams. A high impact team is capable of seeing when and how it has gone off course and of correcting its path so that it can continue toward its destination. The three key coaching skills for helping teams learn to stay on course are:

1. **Anchoring:** Remind the team who they are (their shared purpose and vision), where they are on their journey, and their stated goals and objectives. Anchor the team when they meet a milestone, when they make a transition from one phase of development to the next, or when the boat needs work! In its simplest terms, this means telling team members, "You were here then . . . You are here now (or you are not here) . . . This is where you will be soon."

2. **Drawing Distinctions:** Help the team discern their current position and what's needed now. Do you need this or do you need that? Are you off course, or are you feeling off course because you've entered a new phase? Are you controlling or are you in charge?

3. **Clarifying:** Clarify the intention of the current actions. You might challenge the team with questions like "If you looked at your situation a little more broadly, what would you see? What are you really trying to achieve now? How do you know that? I heard you saying X, is that what you meant to convey? I hear your interpretation; what are the facts?"

> When one door of happiness closes, another opens; but often we look so long at the closed door that we do not see the one which has been opened for us.
>
> – Helen Keller

TREASURE CHEST ACTIVITY: STORYBOARDING

Stories help us learn. A storyboard is a visual representation of the story of the team's work or journey. A storyboard can be a mural in the team's "war room," a cartoon representation of its work together, or a multimedia montage of the team's journey. It includes a timeline of the team's work, its purpose and vision, key milestones, conflicts and changes that have occurred, decisions to be made, the crew and stakeholders, and resources to be added or taken away.

Teams who tap into their creativity to create the storyboard foster collaboration, infuse creativity, and renew energy. The team can even employ an artist to create its storyboard. See Figure 1 for an example of a storyboard that served as one team's visual image of their journey to high performance.

How will your team capture and convey its story?

Benefits of Creating a Storyboard

- Storyboards tell the team's story to executives, new team members, and customers.
- Storyboards document progress and keep targets in focus.
- Storyboarding is a creative activity that personifies and revitalizes the team's tasks.
- For large teams, the storyboard is a way for sub-teams to see how their work contributes to the overall target and to learn of the contributions of other teams.
- Storyboarding is an innovative method for reflecting on problems and obstacles before they occur.

The Quest

Figure 1: One Team's Journey to High Impact

CASE STORY: AT WIT'S END WITH CONFLICT
The Situation

Cindy and Thomas were clearly at each other's throats. Thomas was the team leader for Company A; he hired Cindy's company (Company B) to consult for a large technology project. The crew was composed of team members from both Company A and Company B. Six months into the project, when the relationship between Cindy and Thomas was reaching gale force, we were engaged to coach the team.

When we started the engagement, the conflict was so intense that they had refused to be in the room with each other. What we learned in our intake interviews was that Thomas is a directive leader while Cindy is a relationship-building leader. Not surprisingly, vital parts of the project were far behind schedule.

Coaching Strategies

To gain significant headway with this team, we began at the helm by addressing the leadership conflict between the leaders. Both Cindy and Thomas agreed to participate. We created a safe environment by gaining their agreement to see the conflict through, setting ground rules, and stating that the meeting would be adjourned if these agreements were broken.

> "This is what I heard . . . Is this what you are trying to tell me?"

Each person had the same amount of time to speak. We agreed to sit quietly if the time wasn't used and to cut off the speaking at the allotted time. Each person agreed to listen without interrupting. There would be no loud voices and each person was expected to look at the other person while they were speaking. They committed to stick to this process until it was complete and to set a meeting to follow up on agreements made in the process.

Each leader had time to tell his or her side of the story about the conflict. When the story was complete, the other leader confirmed what they heard to ensure the story was conveyed as intended.

Next, each leader had three minutes to make requests of the other leader. They then collaborated on a joint solution. At the point of collaboration, the weight of the conflict started to lift. Both agreed to change their behaviors. Thomas agreed to strategize with Cindy prior to each meeting, and Cindy agreed to facilitate the meeting all the way through to its completion rather than abdicating leadership mid-course. Both agreed that the changes were achievable, it wouldn't be easy, and they would determinedly pursue the negotiated changes. In their follow-up meeting one week later, they discussed some of the challenges, fine-tuned their working agreement and even acknowledged each other for the changes made.

In recapping the resolution they had forged, Cindy said she felt heard. Thomas said that he was glad they had a way of clearing the air between them. "It's so much easier to come to work," Thomas said. Cindy responded, "We don't want to hold onto hard feelings and we now have a way to resolve our differences."

Because of the impact this conflict had on the team, they agreed to communicate to the team their commitment to the evolution of the partnership.

DISTINCTIONS
Nominal Team v. High Impact Team

A nominal team is a group of people working towards a common goal without commitment to developing the Top 10 HIT Practices. They just want to get through the work and get it done.

A high impact team has developed the Top 10 HIT Practices. Their work is enjoyable, effective, and productive. Team members review process and results and all team members are committed to generating high performance results—and taking the steps required to achieve them.

Communicate v. Relate

To communicate is to exchange or pass along information. To relate is to communicate with a sense of connection to the other, using understanding and awareness of a personal relationship. Communication relays facts and information to team members and stakeholders. However, relating is a high impact form of communication, since its intention is to deepen the connection between the sender and the receiver.

INQUIRY

Where is your team in its journey?

What is the gap between where you are and where you want to be?

CHAPTER 5

Stocking the Boat:
Preparing to Set Sail

Vision is the link between dream and action. A Vision must capture people's hearts. Without a goal, neither companies nor people get anywhere. But when people have a vision, they are motivated to make it a reality.

—Peter Senge
MIT Sloane School of Management

Now that you are clear about who's on the team, it's time to prepare for the team's journey. In this chapter we examine the practices of Shared Purpose and Vision, Shared Leadership, Active Sponsorship and creating a Working Agreement.

Crafting a statement of Shared Purpose and Vision helps your team get much-needed answers to the basic human and business questions: Why are we here? Where do we hope to end up? An activity is explained in this chapter to help your teams create their own purpose and vision.

Teams excel when their members abide by a clear set of working agreements. Working agreements define how the crew will work together and support one another. Working agreements foster team progress by providing a structure to support the work of a team and to ease the entry and integration of new team members. Developing a working agreement by using the Five-Step Contracting Process facilitates the interaction between team members as they attempt to understand what life on the team is all about.

THE COACH'S CONTRACT WITH
THE CAPTAIN AND THE CREW

It is essential for the team sponsor, the team leader and the team coach to develop a strong relationship that serves the team's objectives. This team holds the first contracting conversation to discuss and come to consensus on questions such as "What is our vision of the future desired state and how will we work together to get there?" Use the Five-Step Contracting Process described later in this chapter to reach alignment and agreement.

PREPARE YOURSELF, CAPTAIN!

Leaders who are clear about their vision for the team and their own leadership are infinitely more effective than those leaders who are not. If you are a team leader, a coach can help you do this. You can also do it yourself. Take the time to clarify your answers to these questions:

> If you don't know where you're going, you'll end up somewhere else.

- What is your vision for the team?

- How do you want to see the team work together to meet the team's business objective?

- In practical business terms, what does success look like?

Example: "What I see is that our team gets its work done on time and within budget. We overcome obstacles quickly because we respect each other and have ways of solving problems. People find the experience of being on this team satisfying and they feel like valuable contributors. It is easy to get our work done—there's no blaming or backstabbing. When we are finished, we are proud of what we accomplished and we know that we did it as a team. Others in the company have recognized our work and they think it's good. In fact, we have inspired others to do more to reach the company's goals."

- How do you want to be known as leader on this team?

Example: "I want to be perceived as confident, decisive, and caring (not so angry all the time). I want people to know that I appreciate them. I want to be inspiring and think strategically."

- What are your leadership development objectives for your journey on this team?

Example:
1. I want to delegate more (do less, lead more).
2. I will learn to make decisions more quickly.
3. I will learn to communicate in an inspiring way.
4. I want to develop others by giving them more opportunities to make decisions about how the work will be done.

- Knowing the phases of team development, what activities and strategies will we use to take this team to high performance?

Example:
1. Kickoff meeting to create a Shared Purpose and Vision and a Team Working Agreement.
2. Work with my coach on my development objectives and team activities.
3. Bi-weekly meetings where we talk about how we're doing as a team instead of talking about tasks. Add a process for developing cohesion because the team is geographically dispersed.
4. Add task-free activities to regenerate the team since we're already good at getting the work done.

5. Change the way we run meetings to be more effective.
6. Create a plan for presenting the work.
7. Have a process for resolving conflict between members to keep the lines of communication open.

- What relationship do you need with this team's sponsors?

Example: "I need to get my boss on board with this project and keep him in the loop so I can get the resources and recognition the team needs. I need to include the Marketing and Operations departments in team planning."

THE VALUE OF CREATING
A SHARED PURPOSE AND VISION

A vision is a compelling statement about a desired future. It serves as a compass to direct team energies and to track team progress. A clearly stated and shared vision allows everyone to see more clearly what lies ahead. A purpose statement, in this context, answers the question: *Why are we doing what we're doing?* Purpose gives meaning to daily activities, while vision channels multiple team activities toward a desirable future. Team members' ability to channel their energies and momentum toward the vision depends on their capacity to see that their daily activities and milestones support their vision.

The team's vision statement is the conceptual underpinning for its working agreements. In summary, here are the benefits of creating a shared vision statement with the team:

- Focuses the team's energy on a future state, pulling the team forward and creating clear opportunities for collaboration and cooperation
- Creates an opportunity to align team goals, tasks, and behavior with organization's purpose and vision

An inspiring leader knows how to connect the small, incremental (and often irksome) steps with the Big Vision.

–

The Corporate Mystic

- Provides direction, identifies required competencies, and uncovers opportunities for creativity
- Helps team members see how their contribution benefits the team
- Supports teams to match team outcomes with customer needs
- Enables individuals and sponsors outside the team to understand and support the team's goals and objectives

TREASURE CHEST ACTIVITY: CREATING A SHARED PURPOSE AND VISION

This activity offers a method for developing your team's shared purpose and vision. The team leader or team coach can facilitate this activity. Regardless of who facilitates, the facilitation must gain consensus and commitment from all team members. We recommend setting aside a three-hour meeting time specifically for this activity.

I. **Before the Team Meeting**
   a. Prepare meeting agendas for the participants and ensure that all team members will be present.
   b. If the team is larger than eight individuals, break the team into subgroups of no more than eight people.

II. **At the Team Meeting**
   a. Create the Foundation. Review the purpose of the meeting, the desired outcomes, and the agenda. Describe the value of creating a shared purpose and vision. Be sure participants are clear about why they are participating in this activity. Review what the team stands to gain from the activity.
   b. The team leader or sponsor then describes the charter of the team including target business goals, key milestones, and how this project supports the organization's purpose and vision.

III. **Clarify the Team's Purpose**
   a. First, ask the team to answer the following questions in three or four sentences.
      • Why has the team been formed?
      • How will it serve the needs of its customers? This question will potentially uncover a gap in awareness of who the customers are.
      • What is unique about this team's contribution to the overall goal of the company or this project (if there are sub-groups in the team)?
   b. Record the answers on a flip chart. If there are less than eight people on the team, the whole team can answer all of the questions. If the team has more than eight members, break into sub-groups of three to eight people and assign each group one question. If there are more than three sub-groups, assign one question to more than one group.
   c. Bring the team back together and ask each sub-group to take two to three minutes to present its responses to the questions. Allow team members to ask questions for clarification or suggest additions and/or deletions.
   d. Alternatively, assemble all sub-groups that answered similar questions. Ask them to combine their work into one or two sentences that answer the question they share, incorporating feedback from the larger group, if appropriate. If there is major disagreement on the team's purpose, a longer discussion of why the team exists will be needed.
   e. Combine the agreed-upon statement from each flip chart into one Purpose Statement. Assign one

person or small group the task of finalizing the wording of the Purpose Statement. When the statement is complete, distribute it to the entire team.

IV. **Create a Shared Vision.** This process creates a clear picture of what success will look like for the team.

   a. Imagine the Future. Ask the team to imagine a future date when the team's work is complete and they are being recognized in an all-employee company meeting because they have achieved their great aspirations. Ask them to describe specifically and thoroughly how they are being recognized. Vision statements can be written in the present or past tense.

   b. Evoke the Vision Statement. If this is a short-term project (three to five months or less) choose three of the following questions to answer. You may answer the questions as a group. If this is a long-term team, select five questions to answer. Put each question on a flip chart. Tell team members to write their answers on Post-It™ Notes (for larger or long-term projects).

   • Who are our customers?
   • What value do we provide to them?
   • What achievements really count?
   • How do our customers, other employees, and other teams talk about us?
   • How do members of the leadership team talk about the team?
   • What is the unique contribution this team made to the company's success?
   • How did our team work together to achieve these results?
   • How do we work with our customers to achieve successful results?

    • What lessons have we learned in creating success?

  c. For each question, look for a way to create one compelling statement. For larger groups, ask participants to go to the question they feel most strongly about, and to work with others on combining the responses into one statement. Discuss themes that match and those that don't—this may uncover a gap in understanding. Read aloud the statement created from each question. Open a discussion to gain alignment on the Shared Vision. Identify what is missing or what doesn't belong.

V. **Test the Vision.** Ask these four questions:
1. Is the vision inspirational?
2. Is the vision guiding—does it guide your choices for action?
3. Is the vision clear?
4. Is the vision effective?

If you get more no's than yes's, go back and rework the statement until it captures a positive and compelling future.

VI. **Communicate the Shared Purpose and Vision.** Have the team leader ask an individual to create a communication plan for the Shared Purpose and Vision. Add the Shared Purpose and Vision to the storyboard. Set a date to revisit the statement.

TREASURE CHEST ACTIVITY:
THE FIVE-STEP CONTRACTING PROCESS

The shared vision is the beacon that all members can look to as they determine and commit to a set of working agreements. On the foundation of a Shared Purpose and Vision, you can create the rest of your working agreements.

The Five-Step Contracting Process provides a rich and flexible model for forging powerful agreements. Team members discuss their individual values and preferred conduct. They reach consensus on a common set of principles for the whole team. High impact teams come to agreement on how they will interact to achieve their objectives.

The team leader or the coach brings the team through the five-step contracting process and assists the team in articulating individual and collective boundaries and standards.

As with any activity you facilitate with a group, use a variety of methods for soliciting everyone's input. For example, to include team members who speak less, have everyone write down two or three answers to the questions you pose. Ask a different team member to write down responses for each step of the contracting process. In round-robin fashion, go around the room and invite each person to share one answer without repeating an answer that's previously been stated, until all answers have been shared. You can easily modify this model for virtual team meetings conducted by teleconference for geographically dispersed teams.

We recommend dedicating a team meeting to the process of developing a working agreement with the team. If there are sub-teams, and the sub-teams are autonomous from the main team, each sub-team develops its contract separate from the main team.

The outcome of this process is:

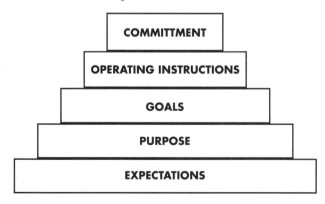

At the beginning of the contracting process, designate a person who will record the team's decisions. The recorder may want to take notes or create a visual representation for the storyboard. Keeping a record will enable you to end up with a document that spells out the team's or sub-teams' agreements.

Step 1. Uncover Expectations

People generally come into situations expecting things to turn out or to progress in a particular way. Expectations are often unconscious and can serve as perceptual filters determining how they perceive reality. Stress arises when there is a disparity between the ways things are and the way people expect them to be.

When individuals assume that others expect the same thing, they operate as if this assumed set of shared expectations constitutes an agreement. This habit creates tension and unfulfilled expectations.

> When a person prioritizes they can relax and stop juggling because they've arranged tasks in an order of importance.

It is essential that expectations be stated so that unrealistic or unimportant expectations can be acknowledged and set aside. Important expectations can then be translated into purpose, goals, or operating instructions (the parts of the agreement). The leader's role is to facilitate the expression of expectations and support the team in creating a healthy agreement. The intention of this step is not to set others' expectations. If expectations can realistically be reframed into agreements about how the team will work together, they can contribute to the team's ultimate success.

Discovery Questions for Uncovering Expectations

- What good experiences are you hoping to repeat on this team?
- How do you expect people to behave on the team, so that you can enjoy doing the work?
- What do you expect to do on this team?
- What do you expect of me as your coach?

Step 2. Clarify Purpose

Purpose provides ongoing focus or direction. It is an extended frame of reference or context within which to view everything that happens. Not having a purpose can be a debilitating experience and cause the team's working experience to be unfulfilling .

If you have completed the shared purpose and vision activity, use the outcome of that discussion in this step.

Discovery Questions for Clarifying Purpose:

* Why has the team been formed?
* What are we hoping to accomplish?
* Why are we doing this work *now*—what has changed?

Step 3. Set Goals

Goals are a way of aligning our actions to our purpose. Clear and specific goals are critical to gain commitment and sponsorship. Teams need goals that are measurable and time-bound. Create goals that give a sense of real, not false urgency. The goals you set are your final performance targets. Throughout the journey, goals are achieved through incremental performance targets. Performance targets are focal points for planning, coordination and assignment of roles and responsibilities. Without performance targets, team members easily get confused and don't know how to prioritize, let alone measure progress.

> Coaches help people prioritize their goals, actions, and wants in an order of importance based on their values, urgency, integrity, consequence, needs, or wants.

Involve team members in setting goals to foster responsibility: this is a cornerstone of shared leadership. When the team sets goals together, it creates excitement and commitment to achieving the target. Goal setting is most effective when the goals are:

* Specific
* Measurable
* Actionable within a timeframe

- Actionable within a timeframe
- Stated with no alternative

Allow the team to raise its concerns about meeting the goals. Having the conversation gives you the opportunity to guide the discussion towards the solution. Frequently, teams state goals only concerning the work they have to complete. High impact team goals also include the development of the team or team members, service excellence, financial responsibility, and improved performance compared to past projects.

Discovery Questions for Setting Goals:

- What specifically are we promising to produce and by when?
- Who do we want to impact and by when? How will we measure that impact?
- What will we accomplish in terms of finance, performance, professional development and excellence?
- What concerns or barriers will we face? What strategies will we use to overcome them?

Step 4. Agree on Operating Instructions

Operating Instructions are the information, knowledge or directions a team needs to be effective in producing the desired results. Operating instructions, unlike rules, are not imposed from the outside. Rather, the team develops instructions they need to accomplish the purpose and goals.

What do we need in order for us to do our best work?

Everything in the universe has a set of operating instructions. The quality of our experience of living is in direct relationship to our willingness to function according to the operating instructions of our world. Therefore, operating instructions are the way the team will work together in order to manifest its vision, purpose, and goals.

When developing operating instructions, the following guidelines are suggested:

- Keep them brief (6 to 8 statements are recommended)
- State them positively
- Be specific and clear
- Include everything needed to function effectively
- Include only those you are personally willing to follow consistently

> Create an agreement for coaching sessions with the team leader and team members.

EXAMPLES OF OPERATING INSTRUCTIONS FOR COACHES

- **Confidentiality.** For the coaching relationship, a key component of our working agreements is confidentiality. Our clients understand that private coaching sessions are confidential. That is, we will not share with other people within or outside the organization, what is said during coaching sessions. When contracted by an organization, we will agree to follow their guidelines for reporting any potential safety issues, but otherwise, it is up to the individual being coached to report on the progress of their coaching.
- **Truth.** My job as a coach is to tell the truth about what I see with propriety. I request the same of my clients.
- **Fieldwork.** If fieldwork is assigned, the person being coached has the option to agree to accept the assignment or renegotiate the assignment.
- **Payment.** Payment is due on time. All invoices are to be paid on time according to the financial agreement we have in place.
- **Feedback.** If the client perceives that the coaching is not working as desired, they agree to communicate this, and take action to empower the coaching relationship anew.

For information on coaching ethics and guidelines, refer to the International Coach Federation website at www.Coach Federation.org.

EXAMPLES OF TEAM OPERATING INSTRUCTIONS

- We will meet every Monday from 10 AM to 11 AM to a) report on progress and action items, b) discuss problems and challenges, c) hear what others on the team have accomplished, and d) support each other in clearing away barriers.
- At meetings, we agree to be on time, to be present and to ignore interruptions (no cell phones and no pagers). Team members are charged $1 per minute late as a consequence for ignoring this operating instruction.
- We commit to raising and resolving problems and conflicts rather than avoiding them. We don't want to be a team that shoves problems under the carpet!
- We agree to do what we say we are going to do. If we absolutely can't, we will address it in advance of the due date.

Step 5. Confirm Commitment

Commitment is the willingness to be trusted and to deliver on one's promises. Before the team can complete its contract, it must assess the level of commitment to the agreements. The value of this step is to affirm the team members' alliance, and uncover what's missing, so that all team members can be aligned.

The leader will want to know if anything is diminishing commitment. For example, if you have just completed a contracting conversation, you might ask, "On a scale of 1 to 5, with 5 being absolute commitment, how committed are you?" If the response is, "I am a 4," you could ask, "What's missing for you to be a 5?" You might uncover, for example, that they feel uncomfortable about the idea of the coach meeting privately with the team leader without disclosing what goes on in the session. Now you can discuss the need for confidentiality, conflicting concerns, and a strategy to resolve the conflict. In uncovering barriers to complete commitment, your option is always to come to a workable agreement or agree not to work together. Flushing out the barriers between "almost committed" and "fully committed" is what makes the difference between average performance and high impact performance.

Commitment is often confused with sacrifice and limitation, which can appear as an obligation, producing fear. In fact, commitment allows for real freedom. Commitment is empowering. It is the strength of intention that supports us in attaining our goals.

Discovery Questions for Confirming Commitment:
- On a scale of 1 to 5, with 5 being absolutely committed, how committed are you?
- What's missing for you to be a 5?
- What agreements can you absolutely not support?

ARE YOU COACHING AN EXISTING TEAM?

Working with an established team presents you with an opportunity for using a different approach to contracting than starting with a team from its inception. In this situation, create a contract that covers just the initial phase of working with the team. Then return to the contracting conversation to finalize the contract once the team has assessed its needs, and set the objectives for the coaching. In other words, you agree to work with the team but you don't specify the outcomes promised until you have a chance to talk with the team and assess its status. Use the High Impact Team Assessment, and open-ended interview questions, to get started. In addition to giving you the opportunity to build trust with the team, the assessment enables you to quickly uncover the strengths or greatest opportunities for improvement.

Information from intake interviews, HIT Assessment results and an analysis of where the team is now in relation to its ultimate goal, will help you prioritize your coaching

> A masterful coach contracts with her client at the beginning of a project and at regular intervals during the life of the project.

approach with this team. For example, if the HIT Assessment reveals that the team scores low on purpose and problem solving and is running out of time to complete its project, you will not take the team offsite for an in-depth visioning session. You will help them learn better problem solving by helping them solve existing problems preventing them from meeting their deadlines. Finally, go back to complete the working agreement using the Five-step Contracting Process.

CASE STORY: INTO THE FIRE

A web development company hired Tom as a project manager. His first assignment was with a project that was already underway and already in trouble. The project was behind schedule and the web developers were heading in every direction. The technical expertise of the developers on his team, the seniority of his clients, and the magnitude of the problem intimidated him. Tom was eager to make a good impression in his new company.

Tom picked up the phone and called his coach. "I want to get off to a good start. This is a ripe opportunity to broaden my experience quickly, but it's overwhelming and I want your help."

In supporting him to clarify his own vision, we started with the Five-Step Contracting Process. But here's the catch: We used it for him to create his own working agreement for his job. "What are your expectations for this job, for this company, and for yourself? What is your purpose in being here as a project leader? What do you want to accomplish and how do you want to be perceived? What do you need to be 100% committed?"

For Tom, the bottom line was that he was committed to having the company's clients be thrilled with their work and to having a team that worked like an oiled machine. He needed the support of his boss for resources and for making decisions that were beyond his level of authority. He expected that he would have the support of his team members and would have to gain the respect of the client company. He became clearer and clearer about what he wanted; then, ideas on how to handle the current project came to him easily. The agenda for the coaching session was simple: help him clarify his vision and goals and then strategize on his plan.

Before our next coaching session, Tom launched his journey with the team using the Five-Step Contracting Process. He reported that the questions in the five-step process helped anchor the team. From this position, they assessed their existing accomplishments and what work remained to attain their objectives. Operating instructions, formerly absent, helped develop trust and cohesion to get back on course.

DISTINCTIONS
Alignment v. Agreement

Reaching agreement requires that at least one individual give up his position or opinion on the issue. In other words, in order to *agree*, we have to hold the same position. That means someone has to be wrong or mistaken. We waste a lot of time in discussion, losing business and damaging relationships, trying to get agreement.

Alignment means never having to say, "My opinion is wrong." Gaining alignment means that the individual can work toward, or commit to the issue. Individuals don't have to change their opinions. You can have an opinion, even a differing one—and still align on the new idea. This means that you are willing to *act* in a way that is consistent with what you have aligned with, regardless of whether or not you agree. Focus on gaining alignment in your team meetings. Encourage the team leader *not* to demand agreement. The whole team will save a lot of time, energy and goodwill.

INQUIRY

As a coach, what is critical to your operating instructions?

As a leader, what is your vision for the team?

As a team member, what operating instructions are critical for you to feel that you can be successful on this team?

PART III

SAILING THE COURSE

You can't direct the wind, but
you can adjust your sails.

—Unknown

CHAPTER 6

Setting Sail

The best teams are the ones in which everybody takes responsibility—
regardless of power position. The challenge for the team leader is
to show that she is really interested in sharing power and
responsibility; it's up to the team leader to create this context.

—Anne Donnellon
Managing the Individuals on a Team, *Harvard Management Update*

The period just after a boat leaves the dock for a long voyage is filled with activity. The crew disperses to work on their tasks. Some of the crew members are putting away the lines while others are adjusting the sails. At the helm, the navigator is charting the course. In a business team, members similarly feel compelled to start working on their tasks as the team begins its journey. During this phase, it is critical for the team leader and team members to work together to continue to lay the foundation for the team's work.

Building on the vision and the working agreement the team has created, it is now time to add the next layer of the foundation. As the team sets sail, the leader's role is to enable team members to develop clear performance targets, clarify roles and responsibilities, establish effective meeting processes, and foster an environment where communication and dialog foster concrete actions. Whether you are leader or coach, your role is to build a solid foundation for team cohesion, and to make the Top 10 HIT Practices habits that your team uses throughout the process.

We were brought in to coach the global leadership team for a fast-growing pre-IPO Silicon Valley company. They had been frustrated with the dissonance in their relationships and their constant fire fighting. They felt that if they didn't do something now, their growth would start to slow and they would lose the chance to be successful as a public company. As a leadership team, they were keenly aware that their ability to function well together had an impact on the company. They were willing to commit time to develop their team.

The HIT Assessment results and interviews told us what was happening in this team. They were missing critical foundational HIT Practices. Performance targets were unclear, and roles and responsibilities were not defined, although they had a high degree of respect and camaraderie. Leadership meetings were ineffective in moving them forward.

Our approach was to conduct team activities to develop HIT Practices and fortify the team's foundation. We first worked with the team to align on a Shared Purpose and Vision and a viable working agreement. We built on that momentum, in a follow up session, to address Performance Targets, and Roles and Responsibilities. The session started with an exercise (using a DISC assessment) to support them in appreciating their differences, thus raising their cohesion. With this new ability to leverage their differences, the work on Performance Targets and Roles and Responsibilities advanced with velocity.

CHARACTERISTICS OF SETTING SAIL

In the early phase of a team's development, team members begin to work together and determine the tasks needed to hit their targets. Many individuals are concerned about whether they will fit in as members of the team and how they will make a significant contribution. Initial exchanges between team members are generally polite and guarded. Members may be reluctant to share their ideas because they may perceive disclosure as risky. A team naturally defers most decisions and direction-setting to the team leader. Team members often ask themselves the following questions:

- Why am I here? What's this project really about?
- What are the objectives and how will we accomplish them?
- How much work is required?
- Will others value my contribution?
- Do I want to be a member of this team?

One of your roles is to discover early on people's work styles and what they need to be effective team members. Some people work best in small groups, while others work best independently. Some work best by creating their own objectives inside the larger scope, and others want to be given their objectives. Recognizing and accepting these innate differences at the outset enables the team to benefit from the strengths of every member. This is the foundation for collaboration: accepting and appreciating differences. One of the simplest ways to quickly understand and adapt to differing behavior and work styles is to conduct a work session using a behavioral or communications style assessment. See Appendix 1 for assessment resources.

YOUR ROLE AS COACH AS THE TEAM SETS SAIL

Consider the following coaching roles in Setting Sail:

- Foster an environment of trust and collaboration—this is a primary ongoing role of a coach. Without trust, cynicism and lack of commitment creep in and make the team's work tedious, tiresome, and tardy!

Trust is:
- Being reliable and congruent in actions and words.
- Being open and truthful, sharing equally feelings and data, giving and receiving constructive feedback.
- Accepting differences.
- Consistently behaving competently.

- Support leaders as they set and seize upon immediate performance-oriented tasks and goals that help move the team forward.

- Use discovery questions to empower the team to find satisfying answers to their questions, issues, and opportunities.

- Communicate in a way that creates urgency and direction. All team members need to *believe* that the team has urgent and worthwhile purposes. The best team charters are clear enough to communicate performance expectations, but flexible enough to allow teams to shape their own goals and approach.

- Be inclusive from the outset. Involve everyone who has something to create or contribute toward solving a particular challenge.

- Help the team evaluate the effectiveness of its meetings and provide guidelines and templates for making meeting time more productive.

To tell denies or negates another's intelligence; to ask honors it.

—

Sir John Whitmore

USING THE SKILLS OF DISCOVERY AND INQUIRY

You might think that we recommend inquiry and discovery so that you can get more information to make better decisions. This would be the case if you were designing a solution or offering advice. Whether you are a coach or leader, you will apply the coaching skills of discovery and inquiry to support people in revealing for themselves the information they need to be successful, and to elicit their responsibility and involvement. *A powerful question evokes clarity, action, discovery, insight or commitment.* It creates greater possibility, new learning or clearer vision. Furthermore, as Marilee Goldberg, author of *The Art of the Question*, says, "The right questions go to the heart of the matter, while wrong questions result in wrong turns, getting lost, and often not reaching one's destination." Simply stated, good questions keep the team on course.

During our careers, we have participated in hundreds of group coaching sessions, staff meetings, board meetings, sales calls, job interviews and terminations, and performance appraisals. We've noticed that the most successful leaders invariably asked the best questions. Effective questioners demonstrated both mastery of their jobs and consideration for other people. This is a highly desirable combination, both for an effective leader and for a capable coach.

Discovery questions are open-ended questions for which you *do not* have the answer. If you are asking a leading question (meaning you have an answer), you may be perceived as testing rather than empowering the individual. Open-ended questions begin with an interrogative and they cannot be answered with a yes or no response. What, When, Who, How Much/Many—these are all effective openings for discovery questions.

- What's missing from this plan?
- Who else needs to be involved?
- What resources are important to hit this target?
- What, if anything, might get in the way of keeping your agreement for being on time to every team meeting?
- What do you personally want to learn while you work on this team?

Discovery questions honor the individual. Discovery questions begin broadly. The responses guide the coaching questions toward more specific focus. *How* questions are more appropriate when specific analysis, facts, and steps are needed after the broader *what* or *who* focus has been established. "How have you seen others accomplish that?" "How will you measure your success?"

Be cautious about using questions that begin with *why*. When not used with utmost propriety, *why* implies criticism and may provoke a defensive response. Asking "Why did you do it that way?" implies a possible judgment or critique of the individual. Try changing the format of a *why* question into a *what* question and notice the how the person's response changes. For example, change "Why didn't that work?" into "What were the steps?" or "What caused the problem?"

The inquiry is based on the individual's interests, values, and desires—not yours. Remember, this is an inquiry, not an inquisition!

Use your skills of inquiry and discovery to understand people's preferences and personal styles as the team sets sail. For example, to integrate a new team member onto the team ("onboarding"), gain insight by asking about her past experiences on a team and her aspirations. You might say, "Describe for me a time when you worked on a team and it was a good experience." Follow up with questions like, "What were some of the reasons it was a good experience? What do you want to achieve on this team?" In other words, ask about positive past experiences and what the individual hopes to achieve. When you make a habit of drawing out a positive team experience, you more easily set the standard and foster an environment for collaboration when the team gathers as a group.

> Listening is the opposite of preparing to respond.

Some people naturally ask questions while others find that developing the art of asking questions requires intention and practice. What can you do to stay in your natural curious state and ask questions that come from your genuine trust of others to find the right answer? We offer the following guidelines:

1. Stay in the present and focus on the person . . . not on results.
2. Listen without judgment.
3. Ensure that you are not attached to an outcome.
4. Notice when you are asking detail questions instead of asking questions about how the person is experiencing the situation.
5. Risk being wrong.
6. Give the gift of silence to allow someone to find his or her own true answer.
7. Know that sometimes people may not like your question and that's okay.

SETTING PERFORMANCE TARGETS

Activities that enable a team to define the work to be completed and develop clear and measurable performance targets will help the team move toward high performance. The value of clearly articulated performance targets is that they translate the abstract language of the team's vision into specific measurable goals and concrete milestones. Only through the development of performance targets and a process to measure performance can a team identify whether or not it is on course. Performance targets, and measuring against them, empower a team to set its sights not only on meeting customer expectations, but also on exceeding them.

Goals are a summation of performance targets. When the goals of a team are clear, they can be chunked down into performance targets. In the case of a media company launching a new TV and Internet product, their one-year goal was to raise $25 million in corporate advertising. Given that annual goal, they set quarterly performance targets for key activities that would enable them to reach that goal. In the first quarter, the target was to complete the advertising sales offer packages, and to have an agreement with a national TV network for viewing the TV shows. In the second quarter, they set their target to have 20 corporate meetings to pitch the offer to potential advertisers, and to measure the success of those meetings in order to refine their marketing effectiveness.

Teams that do not establish clear and measurable performance targets may be focusing their energies in the wrong areas and jeopardizing their chance to achieve their goals. When there is danger of this occurring, the following conditions may be evident:

Establish performance targets with short and long-term accomplishments which instill a sense of urgency.

- There is confusion among team members about where to place their priorities. Frequently, this is a source of conflict in a team.
- The team can't measure its performance or doesn't know if it is on track or off course.
- The team cannot demonstrate how it is contributing to the organization's success.

In setting performance targets, involve the whole team in creating excitement, and commitment to achieving those targets. Inclusion fosters responsibility and accountability for achieving team goals. When you don't include people who are responsible for achieving the targets, your team is less likely to be successful. It is also critical to include people who can make an accurate representation of customer needs.

Table 6 is a template for investigating customer needs. For the best possible outcome, investigate customer needs first. Then use Table 7 for creating the team's performance targets. When coaching to establish performance targets, help the team affirm that their goals meet the following criteria:

- Goals and performance targets are specific, measurable, attainable, realistic, and time-bound. Performance targets are the short-term measures that add up to the long-term goals.
- Performance targets are consistent with the team's charter and vision.
- Team goals are based on stakeholders needs.
- Team performance can and will be measured objectively against the performance targets.
- Performance targets provide focus for team planning, coordination, and work assignments.
- Established performance targets enable the team to strive to exceed their current levels of performance.

Customer	Expectations	Key Measure of Expectations	Method of Measure	Current Performance	Performance Target

Table 6: Assessing the Expectations of Your Customers

Goal	Performance Target	Method of Measurement	Measurement Timeframe	Person Responsible for Measuring

Table 7: Defining the Team's Performance Targets

Before concluding the Performance Targets exercise, challenge the team to evaluate their goals and performance targets for effectiveness. Use these five questions in the challenge. If you check three or fewer answers to these questions, go back and refine the performance targets—this will be time well spent!

1. Are the goals and performance targets focused on measurable performance and are we committed to measuring them?

2. Are they compelling? In other words, are these the goals and performance targets that you will want to congratulate yourself for having achieved?

3. Do these goals and performance targets inspire you to stretch your abilities?

4. Do these goals and performance targets create a sense of urgency? In other words, is this something you urgently need to accomplish?
5. Are these performance targets realistic?

CLARIFYING ROLES AND RESPONSIBILITIES

Roles and responsibilities are bigger than tasks. A role signifies the area of responsibility assigned to an individual or team. For example, Logistics Coordinator or Product Marketing are both roles. Responsibilities are the results you are accountable to produce; they may include both tangible business results and the development of others. Often, responsibility is defined too narrowly as the task or set of activities for which someone is responsible. A project accountant might be tasked with producing financial statements and tracking and disbursing expenses. A high impact team would also say that the accountant is responsible for the financial well-being of the project—a much more inclusive and overriding role. In this way, you can connect the roles and responsibilities with the team's performance targets while challenging individuals to share in the leadership of the team.

Teams without clear roles often stumble on the path to high performance. By clarifying roles and responsibilities, a team ensures that it is effectively utilizing team members' "hard" and "soft" skills while creating accountability for results. Role confusion can lead to poor morale and low productivity. Ambiguous roles create stress that can place a drag on performance and make team members susceptible to burnout. Conflicts can occur between team members due to diverging expectations about one another's roles and responsibilities.

We were once asked to intervene and assist a technical lead and a product manager in resolving a recurring conflict. The Senior Technical Project Leader had written up functional specifications for a new product; however, the Product Manager had assumed this was her responsibility. The stress that arose from avoiding this conflict was tangible in team meetings and it was affecting morale. In a brief conversation designed to get past this obstacle, we first acknowledged that we sensed a duplication in responsibilities that was causing a conflict. In an agreed neutral conversation, they agreed that, in the future, the product manager would write the functional specifications. The technical leader would be the first to review them. Clarifying their respective roles and responsibilities minimized the conflict and frustration that came from the overlap in perceived responsibilities.

To effectively clarify roles and responsibilities as the team sets sail and throughout its journey, the team must know its vision, purpose, goals and performance targets. During a team session, spend time clarifying the roles and responsibilities using these provocative questions:

- What talents or skills are critical to meeting your objectives?
- Who are the sponsors of the team?
- Who is assigned to each role?
- Who is responsible for each performance target?
- Who else in the organization will be peripherally involved in the team's activities?
- Have we covered all of the functional areas: finance, communication with the organization, technology, and human resources?
- Is it necessary to create sub-teams?

A team is dynamic and clarifying roles and responsibilities is an iterative process. As milestones and performance targets are met, changing needs for skills and competencies trigger the need to review and adjust roles and responsibilities. Onboarding new team members is an important opportunity to introduce new members' roles and responsibilities to the team while helping new team members learn the roles and responsibilities of existing team members.

High impact teams have systematic mechanisms for communicating among team members during their journey. They use those mechanisms to communicate with all core team members and others who support the team. Use Table 6 below to ensure that communication is inclusive. Communicate regularly any and all changes to roles and responsibilities. People want to know who's who and what they do.

Table 8 is a template for clarifying roles and responsibilities. The two columns labeled Role and Responsibility capture the essence of the individual's contribution to the team. Once identified, you can more easily articulate the tasks and activities required to complete the team's objectives and assign roles to team members.

Team Member	Role	Responsibility	Activities	Sub-Team Assignment	Performance Targets

Table 8: Roles and Responsibilities Template

MEETINGS THAT FOCUS TEAM ENERGY

People spend a large percentage of their time in meetings that are conducted in person and on the phone. Presumably, the intention of having a meeting is to bring people together to get a lot of work done. *Effective* meetings can also be powerful opportunities for developing a strong working relationship. Yet we frequently hear from team members that meeting time *is not* time well spent. Bad meetings can become a source of frustration, convey negative messages about the team, and waste time and resources. We hear these messages from team members:

- Our meetings wander and we don't get a lot done.
- This is the only time we have to see each other and all we do is go through tasks.

- We have meetings to identify and distribute the work, but I don't know what I'm supposed to do.
- We talk about things one week that seem so urgent and critical and next week they're gone from the radar screen.
- I hate it when we're invited to an "important" meeting to "nail down" a development plan only to receive the huge plan document at the beginning of the meeting!
- It's the same thing week after week—the same people talk while others just listen.

The purpose of meetings is to disseminate information that needs to be discussed, address opportunities and issues with more than two people, and enhance team member relationships. High impact teams raise the stakes on the purpose of their meetings. They leverage the team's synergy to overcome barriers, to reconnect the team to its purpose above and beyond the day-to-day tasks, and to focus energies where they are most needed.

You can make team meetings more effective. The components of and activities for effective meetings follow.

Ice-Breaking Activities

Ice-breaking activities are conducted early in the journey and to start team meetings. They help individuals set aside the distractions of their daily work and life issues. Early in the journey, icebreakers can lighten up the nervous tension of meeting new members and new challenges. Later in a team's journey, they serve to deepen relationships among team members. Artfully select your ice-breaking activities based on your intention for the meeting.

Bringing on new team members is an opportunity for conducting ice-breaking activities. A team we worked with introduced new members into the team by having everyone introduce themselves, their role, and their favorite flavor of ice cream. Yet another team asked each person, including the new person, to introduce themselves by describing their role on the team as well as revealing to the group some unknown personal fact. We've seen other teams collect short and more personal bio's to share with new team members when they came on board.

An intact team enhances team member relationships with ice-breaker activities. Some team leaders adopt a start-of-meeting activity to further develop the team's relatedness and focus the attention of team members who are both in the room and on the phone. We worked with one organization that started every team meeting with an inspirational quote. Each week, one team member opened the meeting by reading a brief passage he or she found inspirational. Following the reading, the team member would relate their reasons for finding this passage inspiring.

An existing leadership team launched a new initiative to shift the strategic direction of the organization. They wanted to develop a more collaborative culture. We opened their first meeting with an icebreaker that would develop relatedness on the team. We divided the team into pairs and gave them 15 minutes to interview each other. They were to discover what their partner held themselves responsible for on the team, and three things that would give the group an opportunity to know this person. Each person in the pair had to introduce the other person, disclosing what the interview revealed. After each introduction, they were given a team cap inscribed with "turnaround team" and they were welcomed into the team as if they were attending for the first time.

Outcomes, Agendas, and Objectives

Team members naturally want different things to happen in meetings and they have different needs for the way meetings are conducted. Some team members won't notice if there's an agenda for the meeting; they are satisfied if the discussion is relevant to the team's goals and decisions are made quickly. Other team members want time to think about decisions and need an agenda in advance of the meeting in order to prepare for decisions and discussion. They may be resistant to participate or make decisions if they are not given the opportunity to reflect on the information before the meeting. High impact teams respect individual differences by providing an agenda before the meeting.

An agenda helps a team focus and align meeting topics with team performance targets. A team can identify when they are on- and off-course in the meeting, thus allowing the team to self-correct. One simple approach to getting a meeting back on track is to say, "I'd like to pause the conversation here and request that this topic be put in the parking lot until we set up a separate meeting to discuss it."

Use Shuttle Diplomacy

Encourage team members to speak between meetings about decisions to be made in meetings and about challenging problems. One team leader we know routinely surprised her team by demanding that decisions be made without prior discussion. When she adopted the habit of shuttle diplomacy tense meetings and delayed decisions were avoided.

Creating a Collaborative Environment

A collaborative environment utilizes the team's synergy to solve problems in creative ways. Team collaboration takes the burden from the team leader for solving the team's problems and enables the team to tap into its collective wisdom for reaching its goals more easily. At the outset, create an environment of safety by following the terms of your working agreement. Infusing creativity into meetings creates collaborative moments. Activities for fostering collaboration and problem solving include idea mapping, found in Chapter 8, and the Green Light, Red Light activity found below.

Green Light, Red Light Activity For Project Status

Teams that don't have processes for creating and innovating may remain stuck in old patterns of thinking. Team energy dips below optimal levels and they develop less-than-innovative solutions to problems. An activity we have successfully used with large project teams to infuse creativity is the green light, yellow light, and red light status model. The intention of this model is to capitalize on the team's talent to solve problems.

First, help team members establish the ground rule that no one is made wrong for bringing a problem to the team. Representatives from the team report on the status of their tasks by saying *green light, yellow light,* or *red light. Green light* status tasks are moving ahead as planned. The team member reports on what is working and acknowledges team members who have contributed to its progress. When a *yellow light* issue is reported, the team member describes where she is cautious or concerned and this is what she's doing about it or she can ask for help developing a solution. A *red light* status means the task has come to a halt. *Red light* issues are to be addressed to the extent appropriate in the meeting. In several cases, we've seen team leaders request that *yellow light* and *red light* issues be communicated to them prior to the start of the meeting.

Focus on Task *and* on People

High impact teams create opportunities in their meetings to focus on both task and on people. Team members have time to relate by communicating about their thoughts and feelings as well as the work at hand.

How can you conduct a meeting where people have an opportunity to relate to each other?

We've experienced many great approaches to fostering relatedness. A small team we worked with opened meetings with a story that started with *"A funny thing happened to me this past week."* In turn, team members shared humorous anecdotes about the project.

Another team we worked with was geographically dispersed 85% of the time. Individual team members felt isolated in the field. In a session to establish the team's purpose, it was agreed that the team was to be a home base for its members. With this agreement, they changed the focus of their meetings to supporting each other. They deepened the trust on the team by relating their experiences and feelings about their projects. They used meeting time to collaborate on solutions to problems in the field.

Recapping

In high impact teams, team members are rigorous about recapping the action items they are responsible for at the end of each and every meeting. The team leader does not recap for a team member. Each team member recaps his or her own action items. Recapping confirms agreement and uncovers any potential misunderstandings about tasks or deadlines.

Recognizing, Reminiscing and Reconnecting

Take time at each meeting to recognize team accomplishments and acknowledge meaningful contributions. When critical milestones are met we encourage teams to organize task-free meetings or more casual gatherings to recognize completion and to reminisce. The team reviews accomplishments, lessons learned and challenges that have been met. This reconnects the team to its vision and purpose and helps it chart its course.

CASE STORY: THE NEXT GENERATION
The Situation

We were preparing for a kickoff meeting with the leader of an organization that pulled together a multinational virtual team. Their charter was an aggressive eighteen-month initiative to deliver TV productions, real-time Internet video, and feature films for the next generation of ocean exploration. The team included consultants from more than five organizations responsible for public relations, web technology, operations and production, sponsorship sales, cinematography and finance.

It was easy to agree on the desired outcomes of the kickoff meeting: defining strategies, performance targets, key milestones, roles and responsibilities, and a working agreement. When we talked about creating a shared vision that would inspire and pull the team forward, the executive sponsor balked, saying, "I don't have to inspire them; I pay them."

It was clear that he had a vision of where things were headed and what the future looked like. We acknowledged him for having a clear vision and pointed out that the team did not yet share his vision. Until they shared his vision, he would find himself pushing them towards a future they don't see, rather than allowing the shared vision to pull them forward. Once he understood this perspective, he agreed to conduct the visioning activity, asking only that it not be too "touchy feely."

During our first day-long kickoff meeting, we started the visioning activity with the leader sharing his vision. As a result, by the end of the activity the team articulated an inspiring vision for the organization. They were then ready to identify performance targets, strategies to hit the targets, and roles and responsibilities. As the team worked through these activities, we recorded some of the concerns that were expressed and expectations that were held by team members. Finally, the team took their concerns and expectations and turned them into operating instructions.

At the end of the session, the recap with the team was the most inspirational time of the day. During the recap, we felt compelled to ask: "What is it about this project that is inspiring to you?" This is what they said:

- I think we've got what it takes to realize our vision.
- I never would have thought that in such a short period of time we could collaborate to come up with quality strategies and such a comprehensive plan.
- I am really looking forward to working with this group to create the picture on that storyboard.
- The executive sponsor, who was the son of the organization's founder, said, "This team has preserved and embraced my father's vision and legacy."

DISTINCTIONS
Accountability v. Responsibility

Responsibility is being the cause of something happening and looking after every aspect of it. Accountability is providing an account to another. When you are accountable for something, you are obliged to explain specific actions or tasks to another. Teams achieve more when responsibility is the first focus and accountability is the second focus. When delegating or assigning roles and responsibilities on your team, be clear about the approach you want the team member to take in their assignment.

Working Hard v. Producing Results

Producing results, and accomplishing worthwhile goals, is not always a result of working hard. The more effective you are, and the greater the focus you have on what you want, the easier it is to accomplish results. Often, the most productive individuals work very little. Rather than work harder to produce the results you want, invest time in becoming more effective.

INQUIRY

When your next team sets sail, how will you kick off the team's work?

In retrospect, when you kicked off your current project, what was missing? What impact do you think this has had on the ability of team members to work well together?

What three changes will you make to raise the effectiveness of your meetings?

CHAPTER 7

Weathering Storms

The moment we break faith with one another,
the sea engulfs and the light goes out.

—James Baldwin

Imagine that your team is bringing the boat over a bar into the harbor and a storm is rising. Swiftly, you approach the bar and intuitively you know that if you don't go with the wind, with the waves, and with the current, your boat will be in trouble. If the boat is hit broadside with a wave, you could capsize. If a wave comes over the stern, you could lose headway quickly, or worse, you could jeopardize the safety of your crew. But if the crew maintains their focus on the wind, the waves, and the current, you will make it to harbor safely and triumphantly. The information in this chapter will help you keep your team afloat as you weather the inevitable storms and treacherous conditions that confront you.

Every voyage includes squalls and storms. Your team's voyage from formation to adjournment is no exception. Expect chaos, conflict and struggles for power as the work gets underway. High impact teams handle these predictable but unpleasant storms very effectively. The ability to weather storms is, in fact, what distinguishes the high impact team from the ordinary team. If they weather their storms they will emerge from this phase stronger. If they do not face the storms head on, they will become weaker and veer off-course.

One of your key contributions is to keep your eye on the big picture of the team's evolution. Your role is to focus the team's attention on finding efficient ways of resolving these normal and expected conflicts. Provide activities and skills for the team to clarify role expectations, manage differences, solve problems, and make decisions. High impact teams develop working agreements before entering this phase to help them weather storms and achieve performance targets.

CHARACTERISTICS OF WEATHERING STORMS

During this phase, frustration may develop as team members struggle to find ways to work together. Confusion and disagreement may play out in the creation of subgroups, the testing of established working agreements, and resisting team activities. Like a boat that loses engine power while in a storm, a team that loses power in this phase may founder.

Team members often ask themselves the following questions during this phase:

- Who has influence on this team?
- Can we work together to achieve our goals?
- What's acceptable behavior on this team? What's not acceptable?
- What is my status on this team?
- What will it take to get through these problems?

YOUR ROLE AS COACH AS THE TEAM WEATHERS STORMS

When conflict occurs, diagnose the source. Does the team lack clear goals and work plan? Are roles and responsibilities unclear? Are conflicts arising from unappreciated differences in communication, behavioral or cultural styles? Is the chaos productive or destructive?

The Three Cs—Resolving Conflict, Integrating Change, and Staying on Course—are part of the team's process at every phase of the journey. During this phase, however, learning to manage conflict effectively is most relevant. An activity for appreciating differences, a common source of conflict, appears at the end of this chapter.

As captain, you foster a trusting environment where people can tell the truth and raise uncomfortable issues. You model unconditionally constructive communication and support each team member in contributing fully to the work. You are in a position to help team members develop relationship skills in tough times. This role is especially vital in teams where cohesion has been lost or is eroding.

Here are a few specific guidelines to foster a team environment in which members can enhance their skills to deal with and resolve conflict:

- Be an objective observer (shadow coaching). Give voice to expectations, assumptions, or concerns when others cannot.
- Identify what's not being said and model telling the truth.
- Help team members accept that conflict is normal.
- Help them manage and appreciate their individual differences.

PREPARING TEAM MEMBERS TO DEAL WITH STORMS

Storms are a natural occurrence in the physical world; they are normal on teams, too. As we've said earlier, if there weren't any storms, we'd have to check the pulse of the team members. A complete absence of conflict might imply that no one cared about the project at all.

Storms in a team take many forms. Let's separate a sun-shower from a squall from a hurricane. A sun shower is like a normal disagreement that is presented, discussed and resolved. A squall might be similar to a leader getting outwardly upset in a meeting because he received unexpected bad news. A full-blown hurricane occurs when there are long-running relationship conflicts or ongoing disagreements about the work of the team. If you were on this boat in a full-blown hurricane in the middle of the ocean and the crew didn't know how to maneuver through it, you'd wish you'd taken a different boat.

Fortunately, there's a formula for getting through storms: Insight + Willingness + Competency = Results.

Willingness encompasses the desire and commitment to address conflict and differences. Competency is the skill to uncover and navigate differences of personality, approach, and values. As teams raise their willingness and their competency, their capacity for high performance increases as well.

Create an Agreement to Address Storms

High impact teams include in their working agreement a commitment to address and work through conflict. An agreement to resolve conflict is a starting point for engendering the safety necessary to raise problems as they occur. For intact teams, we ask team leaders, "If you were a fly on the wall observing your interactions with the team, would you say team members feel empowered to raise issues?" If the leader expresses doubt, we would ask the leader to consider facilitating a team meeting during which team members can reach a clear agreement about how to address and manage conflict.

Understand and Appreciate Who's Who on the Team

Early in a team's development, we conduct behavioral, personality and team assessments. Assessments enable people to recognize their inherent talents and those of their team members. Assessments also help us flex our approach in response to others or the situation. In addition, we use assessment tools to identify natural behavioral talents that are critical to team success. A small leadership team we coached realized they were all driving, challenge-oriented, big-picture thinkers. No one brought the natural talent of coordinating details and executing the plan they had conceived. Two things had to happen in order for them to reach their goals. First, they needed to clarify their roles and responsibilities. Second, they needed to recruit members with complementary skills and talents.

Early Wins

Teams need to experience winning as a team to produce more winning as a team. Standard project plans usually schedule milestones that are too far out to build the experience of winning early in the team journey. Design opportunities for team members to win early in the team's life. An early win can be as simple as assigning three people to work on a project plan to complete in the first week of the team's existence. Or, ask a sub-team of five to come up with a menu of five strategies for meeting the team's goals to recommend to the team in the next meeting.

Onboarding

On most teams, the faces will change. New members come on board and others leave. New team members have the same needs as the original team members had when they first set sail. They want to know where the ship is going, how will they contribute, who's on the team, and what's happened so far. If we leave the answers to these questions to chance, we leave the outcome of their work to chance.

Develop a process for onboarding that enables new team members to rapidly be productive and feel included. Start by conducting activities to introduce new team members to the team. Examples of activities include reviewing the storyboard, past team meeting notes, team working agreement, roles and responsibilities, and performance targets.

We had a client who joined an existing team one year into their 18-month journey to implement a corporate cultural change. Working on the team became very unsatisfying for her and for others who joined when she joined. Her desk was located on a different floor from the rest of her teammates because they hadn't planned for a team of this size. To the team's detriment, the leader didn't take any action to ensure new team members were thoughtfully integrated into the community or the work of the team. She was assigned three key tasks from the team's project, but was never introduced to the team's overall objectives nor did she receive updates on the team's activities. When she asked for more information and assistance, she felt like she was intruding rather than feeling included in the team. Although she finished the assigned tasks, she turned down further assignments with this team.

Team Tip: Tell the truth faster!

Establish a Process for Managing Differences

Conflict often arises from differences in values, beliefs, personality, opinions, and work and communication style. When a team knows it has a structure and an agreement to address members' differences, they are more likely to meet them head on. Later in this chapter, we share an activity for uncovering and managing differences.

Develop Decision-making Processes

One of the most common frustrations for people working in a team environment is an ineffective or unclear decision-making process. For example, we recently worked with a team that tried to implement a key decision without first achieving consensus. The implementation efforts failed because due to a lack of commitment and support. The team lost valuable time, promised financing, and critical stakeholders. In another situation, we worked with a team that attempted to come to consensus on decisions that were better made by one person. The result: Team members felt their time was wasted. In both situations, the decision-making process was insufficiently defined.

SYMPTOMS OF IMPENDING TROUBLE

Has this ever been your experience?

- Team members say they will do something, but it doesn't get done and they deny committing to the activity.
- During meetings, you notice that some team members always sit together and they consistently don't sit with other team members.
- You hear gossip and/or complaints that there is talking behind people's backs.
- Some team members do not contribute during team meetings, but they have a lot to say after the meeting.

Being a competent team leader or coach means you can identify signs of impending trouble and implement strategies that diminish the impact of the trouble. The following conditions and problem behaviors may adversely affect the functioning of a team:

1. **Lack of Team Maturity:** Teams typically require time to develop and stabilize their patterns of working together. Allowing a team the time to establish a solid foundation is critical to enhancing team skills that foster high impact.

2. **Team History:** Prior team experiences can detract from the current team's functioning because people bring expectations about how this team will interact. Taking the time to discuss expectations and develop

working agreements can help team members be more open to a new team experience.

3. **Mixed Motives of Team Members:** Hidden agendas and unmet needs of team members can slow the boat down or take them off course, impeding team progress.

4. **Obstructive Individual Behaviors:** Individual behaviors such as dominating the conversation, wandering from the topic, directing others' activities and excessive arguing, all interfere with team effectiveness.

5. **Passive Uninvolvement:** Strategies are needed for involving team members who are not paying attention, not participating, or showing little interest. One possibility is to divide up responsibilities and assign the passive, uninvolved member a role that is essential to the team's success. For example, assign the role of gatekeeper. In this role, the gatekeeper asks if anyone else has ideas about the topic. If the uninvolved team member does not contribute his information, other team members will need to find ways to actively involve him.

6. **Active Uninvolvement:** Strategies are required for involving team members who talk about everything but the work of the team, leave meetings early, refuse to contribute, or sabotage the work of the team. One possibility is to assign this type of member a specific role to monitor group norms and working agreements. Also, a team leader or team member can constructively share their observation with the team member.

7. **Independence:** When a team member is working alone and ignoring the team discussion, the following actions may help to bring him into the work of the team. Limit the resources in the team so that team members will have to share materials or equipment.

The independent member will then have to interact and collaborate to complete his objectives.

8. **Taking Charge:** When one team member is doing the bulk of the work, making unilateral decisions, or refusing assistance and input from other members, the following strategies may help to balance the team. Divide up materials so that each team member has information that others need to complete the task. The member taking charge will have to interact and collaborate. Make balanced participation a meeting norm and support team members in auditing each meeting against their meeting norms. Assign roles so that other team members have powerful and dominant roles. Or, practice gate keeping. For example, "We've heard from you on this; I'd like to hear what others have to say."

CONFLICT: PLAN FOR IT!

What are conflicts really? They are simply unresolved differences. Conflict exists when people see the world differently and struggle to understand one another's unique angle of vision. As we saw in Chapter 5, conflicts arise when differences in working styles aren't accounted for in the team's process and in the design of their relationships. A team should aim not to eliminate conflict, but to use their differences to their advantage.

Conflict between team members often stems from lack of agreement or clarity on the team's goals, individual roles and responsibilities, or team operating practices. The activities included in this book are designed to help teams reach agreement on these practices before conflicts arise. For example, team members who are not clear on team goals may have different opinions regarding what the goals should be. Thus, conflicts focus attention on problems that need to be solved. Recognition of problems frequently energizes the team to solve them.

> Team Tip: Conflict is a normal part of working together. Plan for it.

Conflict is a normal, we repeat: normal, part of working together. In high performing teams, team members address conflict
swiftly as it arises. Managing conflict is utilizing differences between people to support individual and team effectiveness. When
a conflict is managed properly, it can help focus the entire group
on meeting the team's goals. Constructive conflict resolution may
help strengthen the relationship between team members and increase their ability to solve future conflicts with each other.

A product director at a high-tech company came to a coaching
session to discuss a nasty conflict between a manager who worked
for her and an employee of the manager. We strategized with her
on using the Managing Differences process outlined below, advis-
ing her to first get approval from her own HR department. Even
though she had never used a process like this before, she said it
went surprisingly well—her sense was that both people simply
wanted to be heard, and to ask minor changes from the other.
Because this issue had escalated to the point where one employee
was pleading for a transfer, it looked like the conflict was much
more complicated.

One month later, she provided us with an update. Over the
phone we could tell that she was beaming. The employee had
stopped her in the hall to say, "I really want to thank you for medi-
ating that conversation. If you had told me three months ago that
I could enjoy coming to work, I would have said you were crazy. I
now feel completely comfortable talking with her about problems
and it's going really well. I've watched her begin to get stressed out
as if she's going to yell again, and she stops herself. I'm impressed
with what she's doing."

Perfect the present. In the face of disappointment, bad news or
problems, we all have a tendency to resist what is so. Perfecting the
present is a process to help team members see exactly how the current time or situation really is perfect, even if it is not desirable or
tolerable. When we can see how the present is perfect, we can accept it and be open to creating solutions.

TREASURE CHEST ACTIVITY:
UNCOVERING AND MANAGING DIFFERENCES

Here is an activity to develop the skills for managing conflict between two people constructively. It is a proven approach to managing conflict through the appreciation of differences.

Before the meeting, talk with each participant to gain their agreement to participate in this session. Arrange for a meeting location where you will be uninterrupted.

1. **Establish Ground Rules.** Examples of ground rules include:
    *   Each person agrees to stay with the process until it is complete.
    *   No interruptions, no name-calling, and no angry outbursts.
    *   Each person agrees to listen without interruption while the other person speaks.

2. **Understand the Situation.**
    *   Ask each person to write three to five sentences describing the conflict situation. The description should include behaviors present during the conflict, how it impacts the person, how they feel, and the larger context in which the situation is occurring.
    *   Ask each person to share their understanding of the conflict with each other based on what they've written. Allow each person to speak for the same amount of time and don't allow any interruptions—people want to be heard completely. Ask each person to say what they heard the other person communicate. It is vital that each person hears and understands what the other person said.
    *   Ask the two people to create a statement of the shared understanding of the conflict.

> Most of us naturally want to avoid conflict. It takes courage and compassion to attend to our differences.

3. **Define a Successful Outcome.**
   - Ask the participants: How would you like it to be? Ask each individual to write down their answer to this question and describe specific behaviors each wants from the other (or their team). Give them equal time to share their picture of a successful outcome.
   - Each individual restates what he or she heard about the desired outcome. For example, "I heard Sam say he wants me to consult with him before I make a change that impacts his work." Participants should know that they are not agreeing to the others' desires; rather they are confirming that they understand the request.

4. **Perform a Reality Check.** After both people have shared their ideas about the nature of the conflict and the possibilities of resolution, it is time to step back to evaluate the solution. Ask several discovery questions.
   - In order for the proposed solution to work, what is it that you understand is required of you? What are you willing to do?
   - Is there anything more specifically required to make this clear and attainable?
   - What could happen if this solution doesn't work?
   - What have we missed?
   - What are your major concerns? For this question, ask each individual to write his or her answer to this question. Ask each individual to share their concerns and discuss solutions to their concerns. This discussion may lead you to revisit and change some of the steps outlined earlier.

5. **Plan for Contingencies.**
   - Schedule a follow-up meeting to evaluate the implementation of the solution and to revise the action steps.

- Ask the individuals to identify how they want to handle problems that arise before the follow-up meeting. Possibilities include discussing it using the process that they have been using in the current meeting, or asking the team leader to mediate another meeting sooner than scheduled.
- Ask each individual to keep notes of their observations between now and the contingency meeting. They should observe the impact, results, and issues that arise from implementation or lack of implementation.

6. **Conduct the Contingency Meeting.**
   - Ask each person to review his or her notes of observation. Discuss what's working and what's not working. Give each person the same amount of time to speak, and request that neither person judge or rebut the other's observations. Allow questions only for clarification.
   - Ask the participants to amend their original action plan.
   - Repeat the Reality Check steps as necessary.

7. **Endorse and Thank the Participants.** Endorse and acknowledge each individual. Thank them for participating and creating a solution.
   - If you performed the mediation with two people while in session with a larger group, you now have the opportunity to ask the group questions about the value and impact of the coaching. Ask questions such as:

     How has this process been valuable?

     How has the work environment been different since you identified solutions to the problem?

     What impact has it made on the team's ability to do the work?

REVISITING THE TEAM'S WORKING AGREEMENT

If violations of the team's working agreements cause storms, help the team acknowledge and address the violations. If an agreement exists that team members will be on time to meetings and this is frequently violated, it's time to revisit the agreement. One approach is to set up consequences for tardiness. For example, one team charged tardy team members $1 per minute when they were late! Another approach is to get at the cause of the lateness and ask the team, "What's going on here? Team members are late to every meeting." Additional reasons to revisit the working agreement include: missed milestones, conflict on the team, and meetings where few are actively participating.

CASE STORY: A WORLD UPDATE
The Situation

Sean and Betsy, co-team leaders employed by different companies, asked us to observe a team meeting in preparation for a team coaching engagement. Their project had fallen behind schedule and their efforts to get back on track failed. This is a global team with team members throughout the United States and in several European countries. The meeting we observed was a virtual status meeting of approximately 70 people located in meeting rooms, home offices, and airport business centers around the world.

Ken, a key team member, was one of the last people to report his sub-team's status. He said "We may have an issue with one of our subcontractors in a couple of weeks. They are talking about pulling out of the project." Sean, from his remote location, reacted by saying, "Stay there until you get all of the details." All of the team members in the room with Ken had a visible reaction. It was Friday afternoon and Ken was headed for a plane home to be with his family for a much needed weekend break. Ken attempted to rebut, but in the end stayed the weekend. Betsy was also taken aback by Sean's abrupt command that Ken remain on site.

As we debriefed with Betsy on what we observed of her leadership in this meeting, the conversation turned to Sean's behavior. "See, this is what I've been telling you—his behavior is obstructive and direct and his approach is different from mine. We had an agreement that people would bring issues to the team to collaborate for resolution but he doesn't stick to that agreement. And he does this to me all the time."

Our Observations

We had walked into a team that had been storming for some time. The team had not made the transition to effective sailing.

The meeting was intended to be collaborative, yet the virtual design was not conducive to fostering collaboration. We observed that the communication was predominately between Sean and the person reporting their status.

The two team leaders appeared to be in conflict; it seemed that they had not established an effective approach to co-leading.

The terms of their working agreement, if they had one, did not support a collaborative environment.

Coaching Strategies

Our approach was to conduct the agreed-upon feedback session with Betsy. First, we provided her with feedback on her leadership in the meeting. Second, we discussed her personal objectives for coaching and her objectives for coaching with the team. After a similar session with Sean, we agreed that the next coaching session would be to resolve the conflict between the two leaders and design an agreement on how they would co-lead the team. We conducted a Managing Differences activity with Sean and Betsy the following week. Because their leadership styles were very different, they included as part of their agreement a process for how they would lead meetings when they were both present.

DISTINCTIONS
Endorse v. Empower

To empower is to connect people with their own strength in a way that allows them to reach their potential. To endorse is to declare one's approval of someone.

Endorsing is giving someone genuine approval for who he is and what he has done. Endorsing is one way of empowering someone. However, if it is the only technique you use, you risk making that person dependent on your evaluation of him.

When you empower someone, you help him grow faster and do his best work without requiring that he do more or become someone different. Empowering practices include focusing on strengths, expecting best efforts, and delegating responsibilities that match potential.

Attachment v. Intention

Attachment is present when you require something to be a certain way in order for you to feel okay about it. In this case, if the outcome differs from what you expected, you feel irritated, disappointed or let down. The problem with attachment is that it makes the way you feel at the end of the day dependent on someone or some thing outside of your self. Symptoms of attachment are apparent in the way you present yourself or your ideas. For example, if you find yourself emotionally dependent on the outcome of a situation, you will present your ideas or opinion forcefully or with emotionality beyond the needs of the situation.

With intention you can be just as committed to an outcome; you can work just as vigorously to bring it about; and you can really want it to happen. The difference is that you do not judge who you are by the outcome. Your identity is not at stake. Intention leaves you free to focus your energy to produce a result, while letting go of the emotional need to control the outcome. That's not to say you will like the outcome or that it's what you intended, but it does free you to use the feedback from the outcome to affect your next action.

INQUIRY

What will it take for you to have the courage to compassionately get to the bottom of the conflict in your team without feeling threatened?

As a leader, how do you want to be perceived as you maneuver your team through the storms? (We recommend you identify three adjectives.)

Think of a time when you faced a conflict and it turned out well. Now think of a time when you addressed a conflict and it didn't turn out so well. What was different in how you approached each situation?

CHAPTER 8

Effective Sailing

To reach a port, we must sail—sail, not
tie at anchor—sail, not drift.

—Franklin Delano Roosevelt

If your team has learned to weather the initial storms well, it will enter a period of smooth sailing. Telltale signs of a team that can effectively sail together include meeting early milestones while collaboration and synergy are high. High impact teams find ways to balance their energies between completing the work of the team and developing relationships with each other and with other teams.

During this phase, your role is to help your team stay on course. Just as a navigator on a boat continues to be vigilant even after the boat is sailing on course, the coach must stay alert to subtle indicators of the team's progress. Listen for and acknowledge the team when you notice that they are meeting performance targets while building collaboration.

Be aware of signs of unresolved discord. Veering off-course

typically occurs after the team has weathered a few storms and is not prepared to weather more. Team members may become complacent or fall into comfortable routines. As critical deadlines loom, unexpected expressions of stress may also arise. Leaders may have become deeply engaged in delegating and managing tasks at the expense of neglecting important relations with other teams or sponsors. Your role is to create and seize opportunities for renewal and to help the team improve relations with other teams or stakeholders.

CHARACTERISTICS OF EFFECTIVE SAILING

In this phase team members continue to build team esteem as they work together. The time spent hammering out agreements, clarifying responsibilities and learning to weather storms now pays off as team members interact with one another constructively. Team pride and camaraderie are evident. Teams have a tendency to focus on issues inside the team during this stage, and it is important to remind them to cultivate relationships with other teams in the larger organization to ensure that the team's work integrates smoothly into the larger picture.

Like the course of a boat, the team's journey will not follow a perfectly straight line from beginning to end. A high performing team can enter stormy weather at any time, particularly when the team is under extreme pressure, when things are not going as well as expected, or priorities change. At this stage, the ability to do the third C—Staying on Course—becomes ever more critical.

Team members often ask themselves the following questions during this phase:
- How do we sustain our momentum and not burn out?
- What do we need to do to meet our deadlines?
- How do we collaborate and utilize the talent on the team to solve problems?
- Who else can we involve?
- What's next?

In order to support the team in continuing to sail effectively, you will need to rely heavily on discovery, truth telling, and developing leadership skills. In addition, this is where the team needs coaching about managing its image in the company and ensuring that it is able to operate interdependently with other teams. The high performance achieved in this stage can be short-lived if your team does not take steps to renew itself. Infusing creativity and celebration are prime examples of a team renewing its energy.

ROLE OF THE COACH DURING EFFECTIVE SAILING

Your primary role is to support your team in maintaining the balance between focusing on people and focusing on tasks. Focusing on tasks comes effortlessly for many professionals. However, learning to complement the focus on task with a focus on people often requires coaching. Here's how you do this:

- Coach leaders to raise their competence and confidence to have a positive impact on the team.
- Identify opportunities for completing project milestones, presenting the deliverables while celebrating successes and applying lessons learned.
- Enhance trust and relatedness within the team and with other teams. This is particularly critical when your team is geographically dispersed. Integrate some of the icebreaking activities presented in Chapter 6 and consider adapting them for written as well as verbal communication on team calls.
- Act as a sounding board for the team. Provide feedback on personal performance and enhance shared leadership and interpersonal skills.
- Hold the vision for and capture focus for important objectives by using the coaching skill of anchoring.
- Tell the truth about what you see that could cause

Celebrating: A coach's role is to lighten a person's intellectual and emotional burdens, enabling a shift from great effort to mastery. Celebrating what is makes it easier to meet the future.

the team's derailment. Identify where the team is not effective.

• Celebrate behaviors that are congruent with true synergy and high performance. Identify skills that the group naturally performs at a high level.

TREASURE CHEST ACTIVITY:
WATCHTOWER FOR OPPORTUNITY

The coach's role as tactician on a high impact team journey is to watch the weather and sea. In other words, watch the working environment for conditions that foster or threaten high performance. In this role, regularly ask, "What's present and what's missing?"

The Watchtower for Opportunity Checklist (Figure 2) is a strategic assessment. It provides information about how the team is performing. Combined with your observations about the team's progress toward meeting its objectives, feedback from the checklist can illuminate critical coaching opportunities, and strengths to leverage for the duration of the journey.

You have two options for using this assessment with your team. You could distribute the checklist to individual team members and collate the results after they submit them to you anonymously. Alternatively, you could schedule a team meeting and have the team members collaboratively complete the checklist for the team.

Watchtower for Opportunity Checklist

For each characteristic, note where your business team is performing along the continuum from low performance to high impact.

To score, collate the responses from the team and plot them on a blank assessment. Identify the themes that are closest to the nominal side of the continuum, and the themes that are on the high performing side of the continuum.

Leadership? .... Ineffective |—|—|—|—| Effective
Communication? (e-mail and verbal) ..... Damaging |—|—|—|—| Respectful
Mood and Morale? .... Heavy |—|—|—|—| Light
Problem solving? .... Blaming |—|—|—|—| Creative
Complaints? .... Hidden |—|—|—|—| Openly Addressed
Absentee/Turnover? .... High |—|—|—|—| Low
Relations With Other Teams? .... Strained |—|—|—|—| Collaborative
Stakeholder Involvement? .... Non-existent |—|—|—|—| Active
Executive Sponsorship? .... Absent |—|—|—|—| Committed
Individual Contribution? .... Resistant |—|—|—|—| Engaged
High Performance? .... Ignored |—|—|—|—| Endorsed
Milestones? .... Missed |—|—|—|—| On-time
Meetings? .... Compliant |—|—|—|—| Productive
Shared Vision & Purpose? .... Unknown/Unclear |—|—|—|—| Aligned w/ behaviors
Goals and Objectives? .... Non-specific |—|—|—|—| Clear and Relevant
Roles and Responsibilities? .... Shifting |—|—|—|—| Clear and shared
Resources? (capital, space, people) .... Lack |—|—|—|—| Appropriate
Team Members Feeling? .... Excluded |—|—|—|—| Included
Reward & Recognition? .... Inconsistent |—|—|—|—| Performance-related
Honoring Time? .... Late |—|—|—|—| On-time
Individual & Team Contributions? .... Not Recognized |—|—|—|—| Celebrated
Trust .... Absent |—|—|—|—| Abundant

Figure 2: Watchtower for Opportunities Checklist

Scoring and Coaching Strategies

Develop coaching strategies that move the collective perception of performance from the Nominal side to the High Impact side of the continuum. Moreover, use strategies that meet the current need of the team relative to where they are along their journey. For example, if you are ten months into a twelve-month project, your coaching strategy might be to enhance the team's Effective Problem Solving process or develop the HIT Practice of Synergistic Collaboration and Innovation. You are probably not going to take the team off site for creating a Shared Purpose and Vision, and setting Measurable Performance Targets and Definable Goals.

THE NEED FOR RENEWAL

Teams cannot perform at optimal levels indefinitely. To sustain its excellence, your team must regularly find ways to renew its energies. Teams that do not make an effort to renew their energy often suffer from boredom and burnout. Poor morale, as a result of either, negatively impacts productivity. Team members will be stuck and unable or unwilling to help one another overcome obstacles. Our experience shows that these problems are more likely to plague teams whose charters call for them to work together for periods of time longer than six months.

Recognizing the contributions and achievements of team members is energizing for teams and sustains momentum. Here are other approaches to support a team in renewing its energies:

> "I'm working 110% and I don't know how long I can keep this up before hitting the wall."

- Lighten up and add appropriate humor when team members are exhibiting signs of stress. Signs that someone is experiencing the effects of stress include tunnel vision, loss of sense of humor, and making "all" or "none" statements.

- If a team member is overreacting to situations they face, help them replace the unhealthy reactions with healthy responses. On a team project, a deadline was potentially going to be missed because of an oversight by a team member. One team member reacted with blaming gossip to other team members. Instead of engaging in the gossip, his teammate simply asked, "How can we investigate this and find out what's really going on?"

- Help team members find time to take care of themselves in ways that will provide renewal. During intense

work periods, people tend to let go of non-work related activities and relationships that nurture and re-
fresh us. Ensure that team members take the personal
time off they need to renew themselves.

- Periodically schedule team outings or team sessions
  that are free of task work. Achieving a critical milestone or during long stretches of intense work are op-
  portune times for task-free team sessions and outings.
- Offer one-on-one coaching as a strategy to help people
  renew. A coach acts as an objective, yet empathetic
  confidant. Coaching can be used during periods of stress
  to lighten the burden and to clear away the fog of stress.

TREASURE CHEST ACTIVITY: OPPORTUNITIES FOR CELEBRATION

High impact teams celebrate regularly. Standards (how,
when, and why) for these practices are established early on
and can be included in the working agreement. While "celebrating" connotes funny hats, streamers and a party, celebration is just as valuable in the form of acknowledgment,
applause, or sharing of positive feedback from customers, sponsors, peers, and team members. One team we worked with included
the positive accolades received from internal new product demon-
strations at the end of status reports distributed to the entire team.

Celebrations, recognition, and reward help teams to:

- Facilitate transition from one phase to another
- Raise and sustain a synergistic and light morale
- Give attention to meaningful moments in the team's
  life
- Reinforce team values, goals, and working agreements
- Increase shared purpose, pride, and accomplishment
- Motivate team members after long periods of intense
  work

> What or
> who will
> your team
> celebrate?

Work with your team to identify your team's meaningful opportunities and the budget for celebrations. Here is a list of opportunities to celebrate:

- Solving a challenging problem
- Implementing an innovative solution to a problem
- People joining or leaving the team
- Birthdays
- Outstanding collaborative efforts of team members
- Reaching critical milestones

INFUSING CREATIVITY AS A MEANS OF RENEWAL

Infusing creativity is another way to revive the collaborative and synergistic energy that was present when the team first started its work. Creativity can break up old thinking patterns and perspectives. Creativity enables us to address new problems with new solutions.

Creative thinking requires periods of inspiration and relaxed activities. Team members get stale and will struggle to remain creative through intense periods of work. Activities for infusing creativity do not have to be time-consuming or expensive. When we were working on this book, we were getting tired from juggling writing while supporting our clients in reaching their goals. Fatigue worsened toward the end of the manuscript as our deadline approached. We would take walks in the desert or by the ocean where we each live, have lunch in a nice restaurant unexpectedly, or go for a run.

With a team that had an influx of new team members one year into a three-year journey, we used a creative activity for bringing new members on board. The charter of the team was to build a new organization to provide operational services for multiple divisions of a recently merged organization. We laid out colored paper, crayons, glitter, glue, sequins and the like. We asked team members to draw a picture of their personal legacy to the team. In this group of 50, many people first said, "I can't draw!"

At the end of the meeting, we each presented our pictures and the story of our legacy. Even months later, we continued to hear team members saying in the corridors, "I can't remember your name, but I remember the picture you drew in our onboarding meeting!"

Idea Mapping

Another powerful renewal tool is Idea Mapping. Idea Mapping is an activity that generates seemingly free-form ideas and enables you to map the ideas together. An Idea Map helps teams create a broader, more comprehensive solution to a problem or to design a new product, service, or organization. It is a creative exercise that utilizes word and idea association. In this exercise, participants use keywords, colors, and graphics to form a nonlinear network of potential ideas and observations. The activity leads to spontaneous idea generation and a vast amount of information that is visually represented.

Materials needed for this activity:

- Post-its™ for each participant
- Colored marking pens or crayons
- Two flip charts or white boards and pens

Instructions for the activity:

1. The leader describes the outcome desired from the Idea Map.
2. Write in the center of the flip chart sheet a word or phrase that describes the essence of the problem or opportunity and put a circle around it.
3. Ask participants to jot down all of their ideas about the problem or opportunity. Put one idea on each post-it note. Do not evaluate the quality of the ideas during the brainstorming phase of the activity.
4. Randomly place the post-its on the flip chart and connect any related ideas with arrows.

5. Cluster three or four main concepts among the ideas generated by drawing geometric symbols around them and identifying the symbols in a legend. For example, a rectangle could describe problem-solving approaches.

6. Now create an outline by listing on another flip chart sheet the cluster headings with associated ideas listed underneath. Rank or prioritize in an order that seems logical.

7. Finally, write a statement that formally defines the desired outcome to the problem or opportunity.

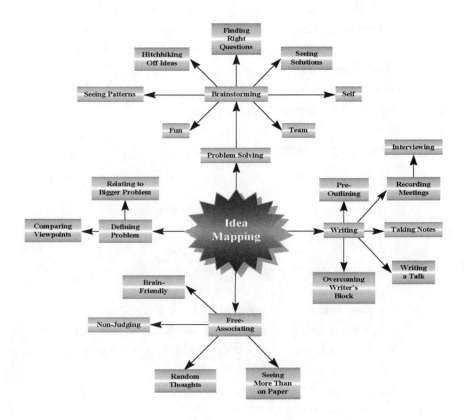

Figure 3: Idea Mapping
Source: What a Great Idea!: The Key Steps Creative People Take

ACTIVE SPONSORSHIP

Strong sponsorship helps teams receive the resources they need. Sponsors promote the work of the team to the rest of the organization; they provide the team with visibility and highlight the significance of their contribution. Sponsors can grease the conduit of communication to other teams and stakeholders who will be affected by the team's work. Because they hold leadership roles, it is their responsibility to ensure that the team's work delivers value to their customers. To jump-start active sponsorship, use the Five-Step Contracting Process with your sponsor.

When employees perceive that teams have the resources and support they need to be successful, they will want to join teams. However, if they see that teams are not perceived as adding value in an organization, then employees will passively or aggressively resist the opportunity to work on a team. Active sponsors kick off or participate in important team meetings along the journey. In organizations that value team and project work, an assignment to a special project can mean special recognition as a valued employee. Team members need to feel they have autonomy while having support and access to needed resources: time, money, and other members. Team leaders and sponsors are called to use their authority to ensure that they have the autonomy and the resources to do their best work.

> The best leaders are clear. They continually light the way, and in the process, let each person know that what they do makes a difference.
>
> —
>
> What Leaders Really Do

In the interview process with a team that wanted coaching to help it meet its annual business goals, we asked the question: "Why request coaching now?" One of their responses was that they weren't getting needed resources from the corporate offices. With further discovery, they realized that they hadn't seen the relationship between key sponsors and obtaining resources. We scheduled a two-hour session using a creative activity to identify, describe, and develop plans for building and tracking progress for garnering sponsorship and needed resources.

QUALITY RELATIONS WITH OTHER TEAMS

Teams fail when they fail to assess and develop quality relations with other teams. Using discovery questions to get at the root cause of a problem, look at the interdependence between teams.

CASE STORY: BUILDING A REAL ALLIANCE
The Situation

Two well-established Fortune 500 companies had been working together for nine months to launch a new alliance. One company had Internet technology savvy. The other company had business change consulting expertise. Both companies served the same marketplace and they had agreed to forge an alliance to increase their sales into the market.

In building their new alliance, they had worked out a win-win financial arrangement, analyzed the value of their combined services in the marketplace, and executed two successful pilot projects. In collaboration, they developed a methodology for consulting and implementing the Internet solution. The plan was to use the methodology from the pilot projects to market to the combined customer base.

As they proceeded to go to market, schedules fell behind. Minor conflicts, previously settled quickly, multiplied unresolved. When they got to the point where they needed to share sensitive customer information, their metaphorical boat hit the sandbar and the alliance came to a halt.

Coaching Strategy

We were invited in by the consulting firm to give an objective perspective on the breakdown. As we interviewed and collated the HIT Assessment responses, it became clear that both organizations had strong competitive cultures. Furthermore, the team had a strong foundation, with Shared Purpose and Vision, Roles and Responsibilities, Performance Targets, working agreements and numerous successes along the way. Clearly they had attended to the task very well. On the other hand, they hadn't fully recognized and celebrated their successes along the way and were hyper-focused on task. Finally, active sponsorship was missing at a critical point in the team's journey.

We believed that the trust built among team members, and the significant success they had already achieved, was overshadowed by their fear that the alliance partner's contact with customers would threaten continued relationship to the original company. Executive sponsors had not been involved after the kickoff of the project and were ignorant of this barrier.

On delivering our feedback, we started by reporting on the team's strengths. After reviewing the Top 10 HIT Practices, we asked them what was missing. They reported that what was missing for them was involved sponsorship, a process for decision-making, and time for celebration. It became evident that a new approach for sharing client information was needed—but only executive sponsors could make that decision.

> Ask the question: Who else needs to know? Consistent communication to stakeholders outside the team is critical to success.

Typically, our teams identify three objectives for the coaching. In this situation, we made an outrageous request that the team commit to gaining active sponsorship before we would address their other objectives. Interestingly enough, they did get the active sponsorship, but a decision to not share was made and the alliance agreement was amicably dissolved.

DISTINCTIONS
Adrenaline v. Vitality

Vitality is natural persistent energy and costs you very little. Adrenaline is a hormone that stimulates the nervous system to act energetically for a temporary period. You have vitality when all of your systems are working completely and in harmony. If you have eliminated things that you merely tolerate, and spend your time at activities that you find inherently enjoyable, you will be vital. When you tap into your vitality, you are able to sustain a comfortable level of activity without dramatic ups and downs. However, when you use adrenaline to meet deadlines or get yourself going every day, your days will feel like a ride on a roller coaster, with highs and lows that you cannot sustain indefinitely. It's healthier in the long run to shift away from adrenaline-charged crisis management and toward developing steadier sources of energy.

Maintained v. Sustainable

Sustainable describes the ability to keep on course and perform at high levels with virtually no effort to continue. Maintained means that effort is continually applied in order to stay on course. When a team develops a strong foundation, its high performance is easily sustainable: progress, innovation, and results come without burnout. A sustainable team culture is like a lawn watered by an automatic sprinkler system. You can enjoy it and you don't have to work hard to maintain it.

INQUIRY

What are the behaviors that indicate true synergy is present?

How can you work with your team to sustain this period of smooth sailing?

CHAPTER 9

Arriving at the Destination

Life can only be understood backwards;
but it must be lived forwards.

—Soren Kierkegaard

The end. What does that mean for a project team? In most project schedules, there's a line item that indicates the team's last task. However, reaching that last task does not mean that the team's work is complete. As the team reaches its destination, three completion factors add up to high impact performance. First is presenting the work. Second is gathering the gained wisdom of the individuals and the team. Last is meeting the individuals' and the team's need for completion or closure.

When the coach and team leader do not ensure that these three areas are addressed, remnants of the project linger and subtly prevent people from being fully present in their next endeavor. Research shows that when people reflect on past accomplishments, their vision into the future goes further than if they do not.

Organizations that seize opportunities to recognize individual contributions evolve, by directing members' attention to meaningful moments in the organization's life. Honoring the process of completion strengthens the whole organization. Team and organizational members experience an increased sense of purpose, pride and accomplishment—and they are more motivated to achieve future purposes. This evolved culture is an environment in which employees want to work.

We find that the attitudes of the team leader and sponsors throughout the journey are critical to getting team members to buy into the celebration process. If they truly see and communicate the value in celebration, acknowledgment, and closure, then it is much more likely that the team will strive to reach the destination.

You can help to create the opportunity for an intentional completion by pointing out to the team that simply stopping an activity does not create a satisfying sense of completion. Team members generate a wide variety of presentation formats and celebration styles once they accept completion as a phase of the team's development.

CHARACTERISTICS OF ARRIVING AT THE DESTINATION

High impact teams work together for a defined period of time before disbanding to pursue other assignments. Just as docking a 60' yacht takes more skill and concentration than steering straight ahead, bringing a project to a successful completion requires expert guidance from the team leader. On a boat, the captain declares when it is time to dock and he shuts the engines off when the boat is safely in its berth. On the team, the leader oversees the team's arrival at its destination. This entails presenting the work, celebrating successes, and moving on.

Individuals relate to celebration and completion in different ways. Some will leap at the opportunity and others will recoil from it. Some will want very careful post-mortem analysis of the process; others want public recognition and a party. Others are already onto the next assignment. The entire team and sponsor are challenged to seek practices for completion that serve the whole group.

Here is a collection of the benefits of taking time to put closure on a project:

- Others outside the team recognize individual contributions. When sponsors give recognition and appreciation to individual contributors, it creates a greater motivational pull to achieve organizational vision.

- Team members identify how they have grown and professionally benefited from their participation on the team. Gathering the learning promotes integration of new behaviors that foster high performance on future teams. This is critical to developing sustainability in organizations.

- Individuals have the opportunity to put closure on unresolved issues or relationships rather than carrying them into future work.

- Team members continue to learn the needs of different team members even as they observe how others like to celebrate and complete.

- Celebration and completion reinforces organizational goals and values. It improves morale among team members and has a broader impact on the morale of the organization.

YOUR ROLE AS COACH AS THE TEAM ADJOURNS

Completing a project is an often-overlooked activity although it is a vital opportunity for the individuals on the team and the team as a whole. Humans, in our fast-paced culture, are already looking to what's next; their work on another project may have already started. The possibilities for your role during this phase are to:

- Encourage celebration as a technology for acknowledging growth, preparing for transition, and identifying new possibilities.

- Coach team leaders on their presentation of the work of the team.
- Help team members discuss and process their experience on the team.
- Provide suggestions and activities that celebrate the successes of the team.

Closure and completion is a two-part opportunity. The first opportunity is for the public presentation of the work—presenting the team's success to sponsors, to other employees, to the media (if appropriate), and to customers. The second opportunity is fulfilling the very human need for closure.

> The only things worth learning are the things you learn after you know it all.
>
> –
>
> Harry Truman

Your role is to help the team and the organization to develop ways of celebrating successes. Find ways to publicly acknowledge the group accomplishments and individual talents that contributed to the successful completion of the team's work.

Members of a high impact team may have mixed feelings about leaving their teammates. If they have built strong relationships they may not be eager to move on. If given the opportunity to acknowledge their experience, they are better prepared and willing to move on. Team members have developed skills that will serve them well in a variety of situations, although they may not yet have that perspective. Activities that help team members articulate the wisdom gained and skills developed increase their confidence to work on other teams.

GATHERING THE LEARNING

How does an organization or a team benefit from the experiences they have had? Practices for continuous learning and collecting wisdom are like mining for gold. One team created a war room with their storyboard, sticky notes, and flip chart papers collected throughout the journey. As they prepared to present their story, they reviewed the accumulated experiences. Their story included both problems and accomplishments. They included insights, interpersonal differences, successes, and barriers that had the potential to divide them. They included activities that helped them build synergy and overcome conflict. Because it was a software development team, they also included technical innovations that resulted from their collaboration. In a company-wide open house, they presented not only the new product they had developed, but also the story of their team's process.

Gathering the learning is an active process that precedes presenting the work. Set aside time during a team session for this activity. Encourage team members to appreciate what they are taking away—what they have learned that they can use as their career unfolds. Teams that have worked together for a long time are likely to have learned a lot, but are more likely to forget their early learning and its impact on their performance in the end. Once the individual learning has been identified, turn your attention to what the organization can learn from the team's collective experience. Discovery questions we might ask during this activity are:

- Once this is over, what are you going to miss?
- What problems came up that you worked through and how did you do it?
- If you were to update your resume now, how would you describe the accomplishment of this team?
- What new behaviors or skills will you take to your next project?
- What did you learn about what it takes to become a high impact team?
- What would you do differently on your next team?

For teams that are storyboarding, take the insights from these discovery questions and amend the storyboard. Consider using the storyboard in presenting the team's work.

Several large projects that we have coached designated an individual to collect information from teams as they presented their work for inclusion in the knowledge database. As teams submitted documented learning, they were publicly recognized for their contributions.

PRESENTING THE TEAM'S WORK

We recommend that teams present both their journey to becoming a high impact team and the business results of their work. High impact teams typically present their work to two audiences: the assembled team and the organization at large. Presenting the team's work to the organizational audience follows the presentation to the entire team. HITs schedule public presentations for customers, company executives, and company-wide meetings.

> Storytelling is the most elegant way to learn. Support the team in proudly developing and presenting its story.

One approach is to coach the sponsor and or leader to ask the team to identify what they accomplished and are most proud of. We worked with one sponsor who reviewed the team's purpose and vision statements and had the team articulate what they manifested. Another approach is to ask the team to identify how their work supports the organization in meeting its goals.

One product manager we worked with was exuberant about showing off his team's work. When he started work with a new company, he realized this practice of presenting accomplishments and learning was new to them. In fact, he soon learned that product development was treated like a necessary evil in the organization. As the team completed functional parts of the project, he sent out e-mails to invite other departments to see the work, hear about team accomplishments, innovations and creative uses of technology. Although he was more extroverted than the developers in his group, he empowered them to demonstrate the products. Their pride was evident. It was the product manager's intention to elevate his team's visibility and recognition within the organization. He also wanted to express his appreciation of the individuals on his team.

As time went on and this became a normal practice, turnover of technical staff dropped significantly. He has since become a Vice President in an unusually short period of time.

INDIVIDUAL AND TEAM COMPLETION

Now that team members know what they've learned and have presented their work, it is time for individual team members to say their good-byes to the team. People want to feel a sense of accomplishment, to recognize their own growth and development, and to be appreciated by others. If there are hard feelings, activities for completion create opportunity to mend hurt feelings resulting from those conflicts. The following activity will help you help your team complete.

TREASURE CHEST ACTIVITY: COMPLETING THE JOURNEY

Use this activity as the final activity with a team that has worked together for any length of time. It generates a sense of appreciation and completion.

Set the room with round tables that seat 8–12 people. For each group you will need one pitcher of water and a water glass for each person.

1. Give the participants an agenda ahead of time.
2. At the beginning of the meeting, set the stage for completing the journey. Share the benefits and opportunities.
3. Designate a lead at each table and distribute the instructions described in steps 4 through 8.
4. Ask each team member to write down answers for each of these questions:
   - What have you learned during the course of this project?
   - What do you appreciate about the others on the team?
   - What do you need to say to complete your experience on this team?
5. Acknowledge what you've learned. The person to the right of the table lead pours water into their glass while

sharing their answer to question 1 with the team, thus filling their cup with what they have learned. When complete, pass the pitcher to the right and the next person repeats the step. Continue until everyone at the table has shared their answer to question 1.

6. Endorse others. Again, the person to the right of the table lead now pours their water back into the pitcher, while they answer question 2 as a demonstration of celebrating the team. When complete, pass the pitcher to the right and the next person repeats the step. Continue until everyone at the table has shared their answer to question 2.

7. Complete your experience on the team. Everyone at the table fills their glass and shares their answer to question 3 using the circular process described earlier.

8. When the last person has filled their glass and has shared their answer to the last question, everyone toasts and drinks up!

INQUIRY

Think about a time when you celebrated a personal or team accomplishment.

Who else was involved?

How did you celebrate?

What was important for you to include in your celebration?

Now, after reading this book, what is your belief about celebrating success?

Afterword

Becoming a great coach or a great leader is like becoming a great athlete. It takes commitment, technique, and time. We've tried to give you a wide array of coaching approaches that you can apply as you spend the time developing your own talents as a coach.

You may be a team leader already working as a coach, or a team member aspiring to a leadership and coaching position. You may have been working as a coach when you started reading this book. Regardless of where you started, you're way ahead now.

One of the greatest gifts that you as a coach can give to your team is the security that comes from knowing that stresses and conflicts, ups and downs, are all *normal*. They are part of the process. As long as you know where you are on the journey, and how to navigate out of them, those stormy days can be among the most valuable days your team spends together. It's our hope that having read this book will make it easier for you to make it easier for your team to see beyond the storms.

Also, we hope you use every one of the exercises that we have presented in this book—at least, every one that you think might be at all useful to your group. These exercises might take up a small space here on paper, but they represent the crystallization of years of work, refinement and practice with teams we've coached all over the world. So please, use them with gusto. And send us an e-mail to let us know how they worked for you.

As we reach the end of this writing project, we acknowledge that closure is hard for us too. We've presented our work to you. Now it is yours to use. Enjoy the voyage!

Appendix: Assessment Tools

*One of the key things that all successful leaders have
in common is that they know themselves very well.*

—Author unknown

Assessments, when used correctly, raise awareness of our strengths and aptitudes and they can highlight opportunities for improvement. For example, we worked with a leadership team that was dominated by the drive for high quality, systematic processes, and facts and information. They were missing a persuasive promoter; projects were completed well, but late. Generating new business was always a struggle. After seeing these skills missing from their team, they set about not only to hire this talent, but also to foster an environment of collaboration and innovation.

Our personality, aptitudes, and our skills make up our personal foundation. Over time and with experience, we clarify our values and form attitudes and beliefs based on our experiences. Behavior is what the public sees that is representative of these unseen components of who we are. Assessments are part of a strong foundation for a powerful coaching relationship. As leaders and coaches, we use these assessments not for the sole purpose of changing behavior at the surface, but also to uncover what lies beneath. We coach individuals to develop long-lasting strategies for utilizing their strengths and learning from their perceived weaknesses. One can change a behavior only when the underlying beliefs are known. More importantly, we will be fully satisfied only when we are fully expressing our true aptitudes and values.

> Model Coaching: Whether you intend it or not, you are a model for others. People watch your language, lifestyle, standards, and skill-set for what's possible for themselves.

PERSONALITY ASSESSMENTS (MYERS BRIGGS TYPE INDICATOR OR MBTI)

After more than fifty years of research and development, the MBTI is the most widely used instrument for understanding normal personality differences. More than 3 million MBTIs are administered each year in the U.S. and the instrument has also been translated into more than two dozen languages. It is used for similar purposes in Canada, the UK, Australia, New Zealand, Japan, Germany, Italy, Singapore, Korea and others. The MBTI must be administered and interpreted by a certified practitioner.

Psychological type is an explanation of human personality developed by the Swiss psychiatrist Carl G. Jung. Jung observed that human behavior is not random, but instead follows identifiable patterns that develop from the structure of the human mind. Psychological types develop as people direct their energy toward one of each pair of opposites. Because one of each pair is preferred and used more often, psychological type theory predicts that the preference will become more reliable and better developed. This habitual use of preferences leads to fundamental differences between people and to predictable patterns of behavior.

A benefit to knowing a person's type is that you can look at a team member, for example, as a different person—someone you don't quite understand, but someone you can come to appreciate. Applications for the MBTI include:

- Assessing team and individual strengths
- Utilitization of the full talent of team members
- Redesign of team practices to match team members' type needs
- Facilitate appreciation of individual differences, plus relatedness as a team
- Career exploration, development, and counseling
- Relationship and family counseling

To take the MBTI individually or with your team, contact:

- High Impact Publishing: www.HighImpact Teams.com. 866-HI TEAMS.
- Consulting Psychologists Press: 800-624-1765
- The Temperament Research Institute: www.tri-network.com. 800-700-4874.

To take the MBTI online, go to: www.myersbriggs.net.

> Skillful coaches work a lot on themselves, first for their own satisfaction, and second to enhance the impact of their coaching.

DISC ASSESSMENT

The DISC model is a language of observable, measurable behavior. It is a self-assessment—that is, individuals complete a set of questions about themselves. We use it first with team leaders for several reasons: it identifies their natural way of behaving and communicating, it highlights challenges they might have with others of a different style, and it gives the coach a foundational understanding of how to coach the leader. The DISC assessment is designed to capture how we act in that it identifies our behaviors and emotions. In this way, it reflects one's behavioral and communication style.

DISC gives us feedback on four dominant areas of normal behavior: how we deal with problems and challenges, how we influence people to our point of view, how we respond to the pace of change, and how we relate to rules and procedures set by others. In only 10 minutes, a DISC feedback report is computer generated and several DISC programs enable the coach to prepare a map of the individual DISC profiles for insightful analysis.

There are many DISC instruments in the marketplace. It is most important to note the DISC is not a test—there is neither right nor wrong, good nor bad! The language of a DISC feedback report is neutral and focuses on observable behavior. Also, it should be remembered that we all demonstrate, to some degree, each of the four areas of the DISC model. Therefore, we possess talent in all four areas and apply them differently in different situations.

Since the DISC is an observable, measurable behavioral instrument, as coaches we are able to focus on the "how" of our clients' behaviors. The DISC assessment should be used as a tool for discovery. The feedback process can be done face-to-face or by telephone.

Although certification is not required, a comprehensive understanding of the dynamics of the assessment and its applications are key! Applications for the DISC assessment include:

- Identifying team and individual strengths.
- Uncovering stress areas for individuals and potential conflicts between team members. DISC feedback can identify work or life environment stressors for individuals and provide insights for eliminating the stressors.
- Work environment matching. DISC feedback can be used to infer satisfying work environments. To identify fulfilling work environments, the DISC feedback must be complemented with a values or aptitude assessment.
- In a team setting, the DISC assessment can be used to indicate the strengths and possible blind spots on the team. If a team has one behavior style missing, then it may have some blind spots.
- Resolving conflict. If there is conflict, the assessment can indicate individual behaviors that might be con-

tributing to the conflict or causing problems.

- Right hires. Profiling the behavioral needs of a job or position and matching job needs with individual talent increases retention and productivity.
- Improving coachability by providing a behavior-based tool for assessing behavioral shifts.
- It's widely used. Statistically validated, the DISC feedback assessment is widely used because of its real-world business application and language.
- Increases individual and team effectiveness. As a powerful tool for self-discovery and articulation of natural talent and behavior, knowing one's strengths contributes to decisiveness and self-confidence. Clearly understanding and learning specific behaviors and approaches for working with others inherently increases our effectiveness.

To take the DISC assessment or to become qualified to use this tool in your organization, contact:

- High Impact Publishing: www.HighImpactTeams.com. 866-HI TEAMS.
- Managing for Success: Target Training International: www.ttidisc.com. 800-869-6908.
- Personal Profile System: Carlson Learning Company: 800-777-9897.
- Profiles DISC Plus: Profiles International: www. profilesinternational.com. 254-751-1644.

360 DEGREE FEEDBACK ASSESSMENTS

Within the last few years, companies have reduced the number of layers within the organizational structure. As a result of this flatter structure, companies are faced with a new set of challenges. These new challenges include leadership and management development, enhanced communication and information flow, understanding team dynamics, and developing effective performance management systems, to name just a few. Traditional performance management techniques worked from a top-down model. In this environment, the boss gave feedback to the subordinates and the subordinates listened. The 360 Degree Feedback Assessment is a performance assessment tool that integrates feedback from boss, peers, subordinates, and customers when appropriate.

Generally, between 6 and 12 participants are invited to respond to a 360 Degree Feedback survey. The survey is designed to gather feedback about how the leader's performance is perceived by others within and outside of the organization. It highlights the gap between what's needed in the role and what's currently being observed. From the anonymous collated feedback, the leader then identifies the areas of strength they need to leverage better and the areas in which they want to improve. In addition to coaching the leader on receiving the feedback in a useful way, the team leader then sets targets for improvement and designs improvement strategies with the coach.

When used with groups of leaders, it becomes clear where there are collective gaps in leadership or management skill, enabling the development of a more focused development program. For example, if you administer a 360 Degree Feedback survey with 20 managers and find that 10 out of 20 participants measured low on clear communication of performance targets and job expectations, coaching and training programs can be developed to specifically address these needs. In addition, you'll want to choose a 360 Degree Feedback Assessment that is customizable to the competencies needed in your organization and one that enables you to measure the change in these soft skills over time. In a skillful implementation of a 360 Degree Feedback program, the survey is administered again four, six, or twelve months after the initial assessment.

Applications of the 360 Degree Feedback Assessment include:

- Measuring individual and collective management and leadership effectiveness

- Developing a needs-based management leadership development program
- Measuring changes in soft-skills development and business impact of coaching and training

To take or implement a 360 Degree Feedback Assessment program, contact:

- High Impact Publishing: www.HighImpactTeams.com. 866-HI TEAMS
- Discovery 360 Degree Feedback Assessment, Targeted Training International: www.ttidisc.com. 800-869-6908
- Leadership Practices Inventory, Jossey-Bass/Pfeiffer: www.pfeiffer.com 800-274-4434
- Benchmarks and Others, Center for Creative Leadership: www.ccl.org. 336-545-2810
- 20/20 Insight GOLD, Performance Support Systems: www.2020Insight.net. 800-488-6463

ADDITIONAL RESOURCES FOR ASSESSMENTS

- Management Research Group: www.mrg.com.
- Personnel Decisions: www.pdi-corp.com.
- Corporate Coach U: www.ccui.com, 800-49-COACH PO Box 25117, Colorado Springs CO 80936-5117.
- Q-Metrics: www.qmetricseq.com.

References

Barner, Robert W. (2001): *Team Troubleshooter*. Palo Alto: Davies-Black Publishing.

Bendaly, Leslie (1996): *Games Teams Play: Activities and Workouts for Developing Productive Work Teams*. New York: McGraw-Hill Ryerson Ltd.

Bridges, William (1991): *Managing Transitions: Making the Most of Change*. New York: Perseus Press.

Charan, Ram; Colvin, Geoffrey (June 21, 1999): *Why CEO's Fail*. New York: Fortune Magazine.

Crane, Thomas G. (1998): *The Heart of Coaching: Using Transformational Coaching To Create a High-Performance Culture*. San Diego: FTA Press.

Donnellon, Anne (1996): *Team Talk: The Power of Language in Teams*. Boston: Harvard Business School Press.

Hall, Douglas T.; Otazo, Karen L. and Hollenbeck, George P. (Winter 1999): *Behind Closed Doors: What Really Happens in Executive Coaching.* Organizational Dynamics Magazine.

Hendricks, Gay, Ph.D., Ludeman, Kate, Ph.D. (1996): *The Corporate Mystic: A Guidebook for Visionaries With Their Feet on the Ground.* New York: Bantam Books.

Jaworski, Joseph (1996): *Synchronicity: The Inner Path of Leadership.* San Francisco: Berrett-Koehler Publishers.

Katzenbach, Jon R.; Smith, Douglas K. (March–April 1993): *The Discipline of Teams.* Boston: Harvard Business Review (Reprint Number 93207)

Katzenbach, Jon R. (1998): *The Wisdom of Teams.* Boston: Harvard Business School Press.

Katzenbach, Jon R. (1998): *The Work of Teams.* Boston: Harvard Business School Press.

Kotter, John P. (1999): *On What Leaders Really Do.* Boston: Harvard Business School Press.

Kouzes, James M.; Posner, Barry Z. (1995): *The Leadership Challenge.* San Francisco: Josey-Bass Publishers.

Loren, Gary (March 1997): *Managing a Team vs. Managing the Individuals on a Team.* Boston: Harvard Management Update (Reprint Number U9703A).

McCall, Morgan W. Jr. (1997): *High Flyers: Developing the Next Generation of Leaders.* Boston: Harvard Business School Press.

Michalski, Walter J., King, Dana G. (1998): *40 Tools for Cross-Functional Teams: Building Synergy For Breakthrough Creativity.* Portland: Productivity Press.

Morris, Betsy (2000): *So You're a Player. Do You Need a Coach?* New York: Fortune Magazine.

O'Neill, Mary Beth (2000): *Executive Coaching With Backbone and Heart.* San Francisco: Josey-Bass Publishers.

Peters, Tom (May 1999): *The WOW Project.* Boston: Fast Company.

Richardson, Linda (1996): *Sales Coaching.* New York: McGraw Hill.

Thompson, Charles (1992): *What a Great Idea! The Key Steps Creative People Take.* New York: Harper Perennial Library.

Ulrich, Dave, Zenger, Jack; Smallwood, Norm (1999): *Results-Based Leadership.* Boston: Harvard Business School Press.

Von Hoffman, Constantine (January 1999): *Coaching: The Ten Killer Myths*. Boston: Harvard Management Update (Reprint number U9901B).

Waldroop, James; Butler, Timothy (November–December 1996): *The Executive As Coach*. Boston: Harvard Business Review.

Wardell, Charles (November 1998): *The Art of Managing Virtual Teams: Eight Key Lessons*. Harvard Management Update (Reprint Number U9811B).

Whitmore, John (1996): *Coaching for Performance*. Sonoma: Nicholas Brealy Publishing.

International Coach Federation
www.coachfederation.org
icfoffice@coachfederation.org
1444 "I" Street NW, Suite 700
Washington, DC 20005
Phone: 888-423-3131 or 202-712-9039
Fax: 888-329-2423 or 202-216-9646

Coach U (Coach Training Program)
www.CoachU.com
help@coachu.com
Info@coachu.com (automated brochure)
800-48COACH (800-482-6224)
800-FAX-5655 (800-329-5655)
P.O. Box 881595
Steamboat Springs, CO 80488-1595

Corporate Coach U International
www.ccui.com
800-48COACH (800-482-6224)
508-533-9012 Fax
P.O. Box 881595
Steamboat Springs, CO 80488-1595

Index